easy crochet
Babies &
Children

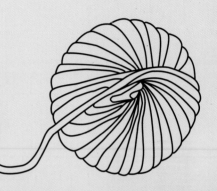

easy crochet
Babies & Children

30 projects to make for your home and to wear

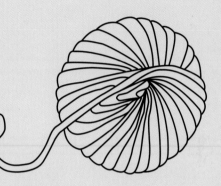

Consultant: Nikki Trench

hamlyn

An Hachette UK Company
www.hachette.co.uk

First published in Great Britain in 2013 by
Hamlyn, a division of Octopus Publishing Group Ltd
Endeavour House
189 Shaftesbury Avenue
London
WC2H 8JY
www.octopusbooks.co.uk

ISBN 978-0-600-62838-5

A CIP catalogue record for this book is available from the
British Library

Printed and bound in China

10 9 8 7 6 5 4 3 2 1

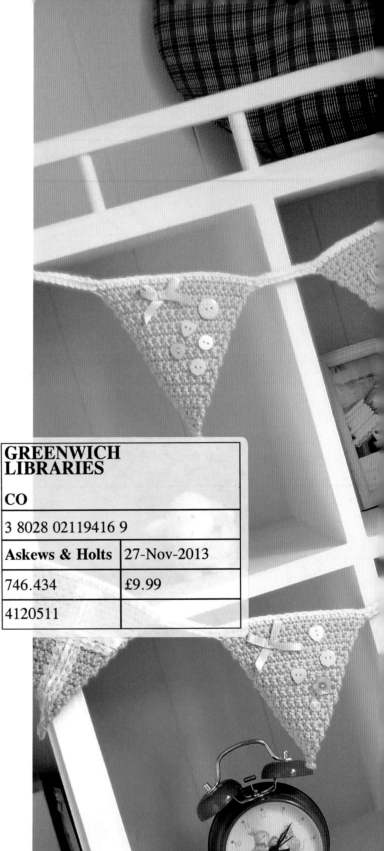

Contents

Introduction

Crochet is easy, and it grows fast. Master a few basic stitches (and the terminology) and you can create stylish crocheted items for babies and children to wear, to brighten up the nursery and as gifts for friends and family in next to no time and with minimal experience.

Whether you are a relative beginner, a confident convert or a long-term aficionado, there are projects here to delight. While your first attempts may be a bit uneven, a little practice and experimentation will ensure you soon improve. None of the projects in this book is beyond the scope of even those fairly new to the hobby. Even the most basic of stitches can be translated into covetable items.

A home-made keepsake for a new arrival or special child trumps many a store-bought gift. Choose one to make from the range of delightful projects in this book for babies and young children. There are clothes (cardigans, hats and bootees, for example), blankets and throws, and a collection of toys, mobiles and decorative items for nurseries and bedrooms. All would make charming, unique gifts.

Crochet essentials

All you really need to get crocheting is a hook and some yarn. For many projects that's it, and where additional items are required, most of these can be found in a fairly basic sewing kit. All measurements are given in metric and imperial. Choose which to work in and stick with it since conversions may not be exact in all instances.

- **Hooks** These are sized in mm (with 'old UK' sizes given as well) and can be made from wood, plastic, aluminium, bamboo or steel. The material affects the weight and 'feel' of the hook, and which you choose is largely down to personal preference.
- **Yarns** Specific yarns are given for each project, but if you want to make substitutions, full details of the yarn's composition and the ball lengths are given so that you

can choose alternatives, either from the wide range of online sources, or from your local supplier, many of whom have very knowledgeable staff. Do keep any leftover yarns (not forgetting the ball bands, since these contain vital information) to use for future projects.
- **Additional items** Some of the projects require making up and finishing, and need further materials and equipment, such as needles (both ordinary and round-pointed tapestry ones) and thread, buttons, ribbons and other accessories. These are detailed for each project in the Getting Started box.

What's in this book

All projects are illustrated with several photographs to show you the detail of the work – both inspirational and useful for reference. A full summary of each project is given in the Getting Started box so you can see exactly what's involved. Here, projects are graded from one star (straightforward, suitable for beginners) through two (more challenging) to three stars (for crocheters with more confidence and experience).

Also in the Getting Started box is the size of each finished item, yarn(s) and additional materials needed, and what tension the project is worked in. Finally, a breakdown of the steps involved is given so you know exactly what the project entails before you start.

At the start of the pattern instructions is a key to all abbreviations particular to the project.

Additional information

Occasionally, more information is needed or a slightly specialist technique is used. These are detailed in notes alongside the abbreviations or included in the pattern instructions themselves, and may occasionally be referred to from other projects.

If you have enjoyed the projects here, you may want to explore the other titles in the Easy Crochet series: *Country, Flowers, Seaside, Vintage & Retro* and *Weekend*. For those who enjoy knitting, a sister series Easy Knitting, features similarly stylish yet simple projects.

Flower-trimmed jacket

Crochet a treasured gift for a baby with this traditional jacket but choose contemporary colours for the flowers and trim.

This classic jacket for a little one is worked in a soft cotton yarn and easy trebles. It is decorated with pretty picot edgings and flower motifs appliquéd on to the lower front corners.

The Yarn

Sublime Baby Cotton Kapok DK (approx. 116m/126 yards per 50g/1¾oz ball) contains 85% cotton and 15% kapok. This blend of natural fibres is lighter than cotton and very comfortable, so perfect for babies. There is a good range of 'ice-cream' colours.

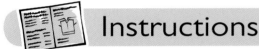
Instructions

Abbreviations:

beg = beginning; **ch** = chain(s); **cm** = centimetre(s)
cont = continue; **dc** = double crochet
dtr = doublte treble; **htr** = half treble; **patt** = pattern
rem = remaining; **rep** = repeat; **RS** = right side
ss = slip stitch; **st(s)** = stitch(es); **tog** = together
tr = treble(s); **tr2(3)tog** = work 1tr into each of next 2(3) sts leaving last loop of each on hook, yarn round hook and draw through all 3(4) loops **WS** = wrong side

BACK:

With 4.00mm (UK 8) hook and A, make 36[40:44:48]ch.
Foundation row: (RS) 1tr into 4th ch from hook, 1tr into each ch to end, turn. 34[38:42:46] sts.
Patt row: 3ch (counts as first tr), miss first st, 1tr into each st to end, working last tr into 3rd of 3ch, turn.
Rep last row throughout. Work 8[10:12:14] more rows, ending with a WS row.

Shape armholes:

Next row: (RS) Ss into 2nd st, 3ch, tr2tog over next 2 sts, patt to last 4 sts, tr2tog over next 2 sts, 1tr into next st, turn leaving last st unworked. 30[34:38:42] sts.
Next row: 3ch, miss first st, tr2tog over next 2 sts, patt to last 3 sts, tr2tog over next 2 sts, 1tr into 3rd of 3ch, turn. Rep last row twice more. 24[28:32:36] sts.
Work 6[7:8:9] rows straight, ending with a WS[RS:WS:RS] row. Fasten off.

LEFT FRONT:

With 4.00mm (UK 8) hook and A, make 17[19:21:23]ch.
Work Foundation row as given for Back. 15[17:19:21] sts.

GETTING STARTED

This is an ideal pattern for a beginner as the basic fabric is simple trebles.

Size:
To fit chest: 41[46:51:56]cm (16[18:20:22]in)
Actual size: 45[51:56:61]cm (17¾[20:22:24]in)
Length: 24[27:31:34]cm (9½[10½:12¼:13½]in)
Sleeve seam: 13[15:20:24]cm (5[6:8:9½]in)
Note: Figures in square brackets [ ] refer to larger sizes; where there is only one set of figures, it applies to all sizes

How much yarn:
*1[2:2:3] x 50g (1¾oz) balls of Sublime Baby Cotton Kapok DK in main colour A – Rice (shade 156)
1 ball in each of three contrast colours: B – Tin Soldier (shade 155); C – Beaker (shade 154) and D – Scoop (shade 153)*

Hooks:
*3.50mm (UK 9) crochet hook
4.00mm (UK 8) crochet hook*

Additional item:
4 small buttons

Tension:
*15 sts and 9 rows measure 10cm (4in) square over tr on 4.00mm (UK 8) hook
IT IS ESSENTIAL TO WORK TO THE STATED TENSION TO ACHIEVE SUCCESS*

What you have to do:
Work main fabric in basic trebles using main colour. Shape armholes, neck and sleeves using simple shaping as described. Work double crochet borders around outer edges using two contrast colours and finishing with a picot row. Make chain buttonloops on one front. Make separate flower motifs and leaves and sew on afterwards.

Cont in patt as given for Back, work 9[11:13:15] rows, ending with a WS row.

Shape armhole:

Next row: (RS) Ss into 2nd st, 3ch, tr2tog over next 2 sts, patt to end, turn.

Next row: Patt to last 3 sts, tr2tog over next 2 sts, 1tr into 3rd of 3ch, turn.

Next row: 3ch, miss first st, tr2tog over next 2 sts, patt to end, turn.

Next row: Patt to last 3 sts, tr2tog over next 2 sts, 1tr into 3rd of 3ch, turn. 10[12:14:16] sts.

Work 2[3:3:4] rows straight, ending with a WS[RS:RS:WS] row.

Shape neck:

1st size only:

Next row: (RS) Patt to last 5 sts, tr3tog over next 3 sts, 1tr into next st, turn leaving last st unworked. 7 sts.

Next row: 3ch, miss first st, tr2tog over next 2 sts, patt to end, turn. 6 sts.

2nd and 3rd sizes only:

Cut off yarn. With WS facing, rejoin yarn into 3rd st, 3ch, tr3tog over next 3 sts, patt to end, turn. [8:10] sts.

Next row: Patt to last 3 sts, tr2tog over next 2 sts, 1tr into 3rd of 3ch, turn. [7:9] sts.

3rd size only:

Next row: 3ch, miss first st, tr2tog over next 2 sts, patt to end, turn. 8 sts.

4th size only:

Next row: (RS) Patt to last 7 sts, tr3tog over next 3 sts, 1tr into next st, turn leaving last 3 sts unworked. 11 sts.

Next row: 3ch, miss first st, tr2tog over next 2 sts, patt to end, turn. 10 sts.

Next row: Patt to last 3 sts, tr2tog over next 2 sts, 1tr into 3rd of 3ch, turn. 9 sts.

All sizes:

Work 2 rows straight, ending with a WS[RS:WS:RS] row. Fasten off.

RIGHT FRONT:

Work as given for Left front to start of armhole shaping.

Shape armhole:

Next row: (RS) Patt to last 4 sts, tr2tog over next 2 sts, 1tr into next st, turn leaving last st unworked.

Next row: 3ch, miss first st, tr2tog over next 2 sts, patt to end, turn.

Next row: Patt to last 3 sts, tr2tog over next 2 sts, 1tr into 3rd of 3ch, turn.

Next row: 3ch, miss first st, tr2tog over next 2 sts, patt to end, turn. 10[12:14:16] sts.

Work 2[3:3:4] rows straight, ending with a WS[RS:RS:WS] row.

Shape neck:

1st size only:

Next row: (RS) Ss into 2nd st, 3ch, tr3tog, over next 3 sts, patt to end, turn. 7 sts.

Next row: Patt to last 3 sts, tr2tog over next 2 sts, 1tr into 3rd of 3ch, turn. 6 sts.

2nd and 3rd sizes only:

Next row: (WS) Patt to last 6 sts, tr3tog over next 3 sts, 1tr into next st, turn leaving last 2 sts unworked. [8:10] sts.

Next row: 3ch, miss first st, tr2tog over next 2 sts, patt to end, turn. [7:9] sts.

3rd size only:

Next row: Patt to last 3 sts, tr2tog over next 2 sts, 1tr into 3rd of 3ch, turn. 8 sts.

4th size only:

Cut off yarn. With RS facing, rejoin yarn into 4th st, 3ch, tr3tog over next 3 sts, patt to end, turn. 11 sts.

Next row: Patt to last 3 sts, tr2tog over next 2 sts, 1tr into 3rd of 3ch, turn. 10 sts.

Next row: 3ch, miss first st, tr2tog over next 2 sts, patt to end, turn. 9 sts.

All sizes:

Work 2 rows straight, ending with a WS[RS:WS:RS] row. Fasten off.

SLEEVES: (make 2)

With 4.00mm (UK 8) hook and A, make 22[24:26:28]ch.

Foundation row: (RS) 1tr into 4th ch from hook, 1tr into each ch to end, turn. 20[22:24:26] sts.

1st and 2nd sizes only:

Next row: 3ch, miss first st, 2tr into next st, 1tr into each st to last 2 sts, 2tr into next st, 1tr into 3rd of 3ch, turn. 22[24] sts.

Rep last row 3 times more, ending with a RS row. 28[30] sts.

All sizes:

Cont in patt as given for Back, work 1 row, ending with a WS row.

Next row: (RS) 3ch, miss first st, 2tr into next st, 1tr into each st to last 2 sts, 2tr into next st, 1tr into 3rd of 3ch, turn.

Work 1 row straight. Rep last 2 rows 1[2:6:7] times more. 32[36:38:42] sts.

Work 0[0:0:2] rows straight, ending with a WS row.

Shape top:

Work 2 rows as given for Back armhole shaping.

Next row: 3ch, miss first st, tr3tog over next 3 sts, patt to last 4 sts, tr3tog over next 3 sts, 1tr into 3rd of 3ch. 22[26:28:32] sts. Fasten off.

FLOWERS: (make 2)

With 3.50mm (UK 9) hook and B, make 2ch.

1st round: (RS) 7dc into 2nd ch from hook, join with a ss into first dc. Fasten off.

2nd round: With RS facing, join C to any dc of 1st round, (3ch, tr2tog, 3ch, ss) into same dc, then work (ss, 3ch, tr2tog, 3ch, ss) into each of next 6dc. 7 petals. Fasten off.

LEAVES: (make 4)

With 3.50mm (UK 9) hook and D, make 6ch, ss into 3rd ch from hook to make a ring, 1ch, miss 1ch, ss into next ch, do not turn but leave rem ch unworked for leaf stem.

Next round: Cont working in same direction and work (4htr, 1tr, 1dtr, 1tr, 4htr) into ring formed at beg of previous round, ss into first htr of round, ss into 1ch of leaf stem. Fasten off.

Making up

Press carefully according to directions on ball band. Join shoulder seams.

Front and neck borders:

With 3.50mm (UK9) hook, B and RS of work facing, rejoin yarn at side seam of right front, 1ch (does not count as a st), work in dc across lower edge of right front, up right front opening edge, around neck, down left front opening edge and across lower edge of left front to side seam, working 3dc into each corner and making sure there is a multiple of 3 sts, turn. Cut off B and join in C.

Next row: 1ch, 1dc into each dc to end, working 3dc into each corner, turn. Cut off C and join in B.

Next row: 1ch, 1dc into each of next 2dc, *3ch, ss into first of these 3ch, 1dc into each of next 3dc, rep from *, working 3dc into each corner dc and omitting 1dc at end of last rep. Fasten off.

Mark positions of 4 buttons on left front border between picots, first to come 1cm (½in) below neck edge, last to come 8cm (3in) up from lower edge, with the other two spaced evenly between.

Buttonloops:

With 3.50mm (UK 9) hook, B and RS of work facing, join yarn to right front border in dc just after corresponding picot for first button, 4ch, ss into dc just before next picot to left. Fasten off.

Make a further 3 buttonloops on right front border to correspond with marked button positions.

Back lower border:

With 3.50mm (UK9) hook, B and RS of work facing, rejoin yarn at lower edge of back, 1ch (does not count as a st), work in dc across lower edge of back to other side seam, making sure there is a multiple of 3 sts plus 1, turn. Cut off B and join in C.

Next row: 1ch, 1dc into each dc to end, turn. Cut off C and join in B.

Next row: 1ch, 1dc into each of next 2dc, *3ch, ss into first of these 3ch, 1dc into each of next 3dc, rep from *, omitting 1dc at end of last rep. Fasten off.

Sleeve borders:

Work as given for Back border along lower edge of each sleeve.

Placing centre of last row of sleeves to shoulder seams, sew in sleeves. Join side and sleeve seams. Sew on buttons. Sew flowers and leaves to fronts as shown in photograph.

Patchwork cot blanket

This attractive blanket is fun to crochet and appliqué and it is warm and snuggly for an adorable baby.

A simple patchwork background of plain and striped squares worked in half trebles is appliquéd with a selection of crochet motifs and letters to create this covetable baby blanket.

The Yarn
Debbie Bliss Baby Cashmerino (approx. 125m/136 yards per 50g/1¾oz ball) contains 55% merino wool, 33% microfibre and 12% cashmere. It produces an extremely soft fabric, good for baby items and it can be machine washed at a low temperature. There is a large range of colours, ideal for patchwork projects.

GETTING STARTED

★★ *Patchwork squares are simple to make, but neat sewing up and adding decorations requires patience.*

Size:
Approximately 75cm (30 in) wide x 100cm (40in) long
How much yarn:
3 x 50g (1¾oz) balls of Debbie Bliss Baby Cashmerino in each of five colours: A – Green (shade 018); B – Yellow (shade 001); C – Blue (shade 204); D – Pink (shade 015) and E – Cream (shade 101)
Hook:
3.50mm (UK 9) crochet hook
Tension:
18 sts and 16 rows measure 10cm (4in) square over htr on 3.50mm (UK 9) hook
IT IS ESSENTIAL TO WORK TO THE STATED TENSION TO ACHIEVE SUCCESS
What you have to do:
Work patchwork squares in half trebles. Sew them together to form blanket, turning some squares on their side. Make separate motifs – flowers, hearts and letters – and sew on to patchwork squares. Neaten outer edge of blanket with a double crochet edging.

 ## Instructions

Abbreviations:
beg = beginning; **ch** = chain(s)
cm = centimetre(s)
cont = continue
dc = double crochet
dc2tog = work 1dc into each of next 2dc, leaving loops on hook, yarn round hook and draw through all 3 loops; **dtr** = double treble
foll = follows; **htr** = half treble
patt = pattern; **rep** = repeat
RS = right side; **sp** = space
ss = slip stitch; **st(s)** = stitch(es)
tog = together; **tr** = treble
trtr = triple treble
WS = wrong side

STRIPED SQUARES: (make 3)
With 3.50mm (UK 9) hook and A, make 47ch loosely.
Foundation row: 1htr into 3rd ch from hook, 1htr into each ch to end, turn. 46 htr.
Patt row: 2ch (counts as first htr), miss first htr, 1htr into each htr to end, working last htr into 2nd of 2ch, turn.
Rep last row throughout to form patt, working in stripe sequence of 2 rows each in A (already worked), B, C, D and E. Rep these 10 rows 3 times more. (40 rows in total.) Fasten off.

PLAIN SQUARES: (make 2 in each of A, B, C and D, and 1 in E)
Work as given for Striped squares but working in one colour only.

FLOWERS: (make 3 in E and 1 in B)
Outer petals:
With 3.50mm (UK 9) hook make 6ch, join with a ss into first ch to form a ring.

1st round: 3ch (counts as first tr), work 23tr into ring, join with a ss into 3rd of 3ch.

2nd round: 5ch (counts as first tr and 2ch), 1tr into same place as ss, 1ch, *miss 2tr, (1tr, 2ch, 1tr) all into next tr, 1ch, rep from * 6 times more, miss 2tr, join with a ss into 3rd of 5ch.

3rd round: Ss into 2ch sp, 3ch (counts as first tr), (1tr, 2ch, 2tr) all into same sp, *1dc into next 1ch sp, (2tr, 2ch, 2tr) all into next 2ch sp, rep from * 6 times more, 1dc into next 1ch sp, join with a ss into 3rd of 3ch.

4th round: 1dc into same place as last ss, *(3tr, 1ch, 3tr) all into next 2ch sp, miss 1tr, 1dc into next tr, miss 1dc, 1dc into next tr, rep from * 6 times more, (3tr, 1ch 3tr) all into next 2ch sp, miss 1tr, 1dc into next tr, miss 1dc, join with a ss into first dc. Fasten off.

Flower centre:

With 3.50mm (UK 9) hook make 3ch, join with a ss into first ch to form a ring.

1st round: 1ch (counts as first dc), work 4dc into ring, join with a ss into first ch.

2nd round: 1ch, 1dc into st at base of ch, 2dc into each dc to end, join with a ss into first ch.

3rd round: 2ch (counts as first htr), 1htr into st at base of ch, 2htr into each dc to end, join with a ss into 2nd of 2ch.

4th round: *3ch, 1dtr into st at base of ch, 2trtr into each of next 2htr, (1dtr, 3ch, 1ss) into next htr, 1ss into next htr, rep from * 4 times more. Fasten off.

HEARTS: (make 1 in each of A, B and C, and 2 in D)
With 3.50mm (UK 9) hook make 3ch.

1st row: 1dc into 2nd ch from hook, 1dc into next ch, turn.

2nd row: 1ch (does not count as a st), 2dc into each dc, turn. 4dc.

3rd row: 1ch, 1dc into each dc to end, turn.

4th row: 1ch, 2dc into first dc, 1dc into each dc to last dc, 2dc into last dc, turn.

Rep last 2 rows until there are 20dc. Work 3 rows straight.

Shaping top:

Next row: (RS) 1ch, 1dc into each of next 10dc, turn. Cont on this side only as foll:

Next row: 1ch, dc2tog, 1dc into each dc to end, turn.

Next row: 1ch, dc2tog, 1dc into each dc to last 2 sts, dc2tog, turn.

Rep last row twice more. 3 sts. Fasten off.

With RS facing, rejoin yarn to next st at base of shaping and complete other side of top to match first side. Do not fasten off, work in ss around outer edge of heart, missing one or two sts in centre of top edge to gather in slightly.

LETTER A:

Left side: With 3.50mm (UK 9) hook and A, make 30ch.

Foundation row: 1dc into 2nd ch from hook, 1dc into each ch to end, turn.

1st row: 1ch (does not count as a st), 1dc into each dc to last dc, 2dc into last dc, turn.

2nd row: 1ch, 2dc into each of first 2dc, 1dc into each dc to end, turn.

3rd row: 1ch, 1dc into each dc to last 2dc, 2dc into each of last 2dc, turn. Fasten off.

Right side: With 3.50mm (UK 9) hook and A, make 30ch.

Foundation row: 1dc into 2nd ch from hook, 1dc into each ch to end, turn.

1st row: 1ch (does not count as a st), 2dc into first dc, 1dc into each to end, turn.

2nd row: 1ch, 1dc into each dc to last 2dc, 2dc into each of last 2dc, turn.

3rd row: 1ch, 2dc into each first 2dc, 1dc into each dc to end, turn. Fasten off.

Bar: With 3.50mm (UK 9) hook and A, make 15ch.

Foundation row: 1dc into 2nd ch from hook, 1dc into each ch to end, turn.

Next row: 1ch (does not count as a st), 2dc into first dc, 1dc into each dc to last dc, 2dc into last dc, turn.

Rep last row twice more. Fasten off. Sew all pieces tog to form letter 'A'. With 3.50mm (UK 9) hook, A and RS facing, work 2 rounds of dc all around inside and outside edges of letter shape, working 2dc into one st at outer corners and missing one st at inner corners.

LETTER B:

Bar: With 3.50mm (UK 9) hook and E, make 30ch.

Foundation row: 1dc into 2nd ch from hook, 1dc into each ch to end, turn.

1st –4th rows: 1ch, 1dc into each dc to end, turn. Fasten off.

Bridge 1: With RS facing, rejoin yarn into 5th dc from lower edge, 15ch, miss 8dc, ss into next dc.

Joining with a ss into bar at beg and end of each row instead of working turning ch, cont as foll:

Next row: 1dc into each ch.

Next row: 1dc, *2dc into next dc, 1dc into next dc, rep from * to end.

Work 1 row in dc.

Next row: 1dc into each of first 4dc, 2dc into each of next 2dc, 1dc into each of next 10dc, 2dc into each of next 2dc, work in dc to end, join with a ss into bar. Work 1 row in dc. Fasten off.

Bridge 2: With RS facing, rejoin yarn 1dc away from point just finished, 12ch, miss 5dc, ss into next dc.

Joining with a ss into bar at beg and end of each row instead of working turning ch, cont as foll:

Next row: 1dc into each ch.

Next row: (1dc into each of first 2dc, 2dc into each of next 3dc) twice, 1dc into each of next 2dc.

Work 1 row in dc.

Next row: 1dc into each of next 3dc, 2dc into each of next 3dc, 1dc into each of next 6dc, 2dc into each of next 3dc, work in dc to end, ss to bar.

Work 1 row in dc. Fasten off.

Sew bridges together at centre point and work 1 round of dc all around inside and outside edges of letter shape, working 2dc into one st at outside corners and missing one st on inside corners.

LETTER C:

With 3.50mm (UK 9) hook and E, make 30ch.

Foundation row: 1dc into 2nd ch from hook, 1dc into each ch to end, turn.

Next row: 1ch, 1dc into first dc, *2dc into next dc, 1dc into next dc, rep from * to end, turn.

Work 1 row straight.

Next row: Work in dc, working extra dc into sts on outer curves.

Rep last row once more.

Do not fasten off, but work 2 rows of dc around outside of letter shape working 2dc into one st at outside corners and missing one st on inside corners.

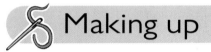 Making up

Using our picture as a guide, sew squares together in rows of three, turning squares for alternate rows sideways as shown, and then sew strips together to form blanket. Using corresponding yarn, sew flowers, hearts and letters to their relevant squares.

Edging:

With 3.50mm (UK 9) hook, E and RS of work facing, work 2 rounds of dc around outer edge of blanket, work extra dc into sts at corners. Fasten off.

Zig-zag pencil case

Colourful triangles combine to make this bright and practical zip-up pencil case.

Keep pens and pencils safe in this zippered pencil case worked in a striking pattern of colourful zig-zags formed from interlocking triangular picots.

The Yarn
Debbie Bliss Rialto DK (approx. 105m/114 yards per 50g/1¾oz ball) is 100% merino wool. Machine-washable at a low temperature, it gives good stitch definition for textured patterns. There is a wide selection of colours.

GETTING STARTED

Zig-zag fabric may take some practise and careful sewing is required for a neat finished result.

Size:
Finished pencil case is approximately 22cm (8½in) long x 10cm (4in) in diameter

How much yarn:
1 x 50g (1¾oz) ball of Debbie Bliss Rialto DK in each of four colours: A – Purple (shade 15); B – Lime Green (shade 09); C – Red (shade 12) and D – Orange (shade 11)

Hook:
4.00mm (UK 8) crochet hook

Additional items:
20cm (8in) red zip fastener
35cm (14in) square of red cotton fabric for lining
Matching sewing cotton and needle

Tension:
3.5 wedge picots and 7 rows measure 10cm (4in) square over patt on 4.00mm (UK 8) hook
IT IS ESSENTIAL TO WORK TO THE STATED TENSION TO ACHIEVE SUCCESS

What you have to do:
Work pencil case in four colours and zig-zag pattern formed with wedge-shaped picots. Work circular ends in rounds of double crochet and one colour. Make lining as instructed from cotton fabric. Sew in zip fastener. Make tassel to decorate zipper tab.

Instructions

Abbreviations:

ch = chain(s)
cm = centimetre(s)
dc = double crochet
dtr = double treble
htr = half treble
patt = pattern
rem = remain
rep = repeat
RS = right side
ss = slip stitch
st(s) = stitch(es)
tr = treble
trtr = triple treble
WS = wrong side
yrh = yarn round hook

Note:
Fasten off colour in use at end of every row.

PENCIL CASE:
With 4.00mm (UK 8) hook and A, make 44ch.

Foundation row: (RS) 1dc into 2nd ch from hook, *6ch, 1dc into 2nd ch from hook, 1htr into next ch, 1tr into next ch, 1dtr into next ch, 1trtr into next ch – from * is called wedge picot, miss 5ch, 1dc into next ch, rep from * to end, turn. 7 wedge picots.

1st row: With B, 5ch (counts as first tr tr), *1dc into top of wedge picot, over next 5ch at underside of next wedge picot of previous row work (1dc into next ch, 1htr into next ch, 1tr into next ch, 1dtr into next ch, 1trtr into next ch), miss next dc, rep from * omitting 1trtr at end of last rep so that 2 sts rem, **(yrh) 3 times, insert hook into last ch at underside of wedge picot, yrh and draw a loop through, (yrh and draw through first 2 loops) 3 times, rep from ** into next dc, yrh and draw through all 3 loops on hook, turn.

2nd row: With C, 1ch, 1dc into first st, *1 wedge picot, miss next 5 sts, 1dc into next trtr, rep from *, ending with 1dc into turning ch, turn.

3rd row: With D, as 1st row.
4th row: With A, as 2nd row.
Rep last 4 rows 3 times more, then work 1st row again. Fasten off.

CIRCULAR ENDS: (make 2)
With 4.00mm (UK 8) hook and C, make 2ch and work with WS facing.

1st round: 6dc into 2nd ch from hook, join with a ss into first dc.
2nd round: 1ch, 2dc into each dc, join with a ss into first dc. 12 sts.
3rd round: 1ch, (1dc into next dc, 2dc into foll dc) 6 times, join with a ss into first dc. 18 sts.
4th round: 1ch, (1dc into next each of next 2dc, 2dc into foll dc) 6 times, join with a ss into first dc. 24 sts.
5th round: 1ch, (1dc into next each of next 3dc, 2dc into foll dc) 6 times, join with a ss into first dc. 30 sts.
6th round: 1ch, (1dc into next each of next 4dc, 2dc into foll dc) 6 times, join with a ss into first dc. 36 sts.

7th round: I ch, (I dc into next each of next 5dc, 2dc into foll dc) 6 times, join with a ss into first dc. 42 sts.

8th round: I ch, (I dc into next each of next 6dc, 2dc into foll dc) 6 times, join with a ss into first dc. 48 sts.

9th round: I ch, (I dc into next each of next 7dc, 2dc into foll dc) 6 times, join with a ss into first dc. 54 sts.

10th round: I ch, (I dc into next each of next 8dc, 2dc into foll dc) 6 times, join with a ss into first dc. 60 sts. Fasten off.

Making up

Using circular ends as a template, cut two circles from lining fabric, adding 1cm (½in) all round. Cut a rectangle of lining fabric to same size as pencil case. Press 1cm (½in) to WS along top and bottom edges and oversew together along folded edges for 1cm (½in) from each end. Sew zip fastener into opening. Sew circular ends in place, taking 1cm (½in) seam allowance.

Sew circular ends to sides of zig-zag panel. Insert lining with RS of fabric to WS of crochet. Slip stitch open ends of zig-zag panel in place along either side of zipper teeth. Cut strands of all four colours and knot through zipper tab to make a tassel.

Child's panda hat

Crochet this irresistible hat in next to no time and make a small panda person very happy.

Worked in simple stitches and practical yarn, this cute headgear for a small child is easy to make.

The Yarn

Sirdar Snuggly DK (approx. 165m/180 yards per 50g/1¾ oz ball) is a blend of 55% nylon and 45% acrylic. It produces a soft fabric that can be machine washed making it very practical for a small child. There is a large range of colours from pastels to bright shades.

GETTING STARTED

 Hat is worked in basic half trebles and has simple shaping.

Size:

To fit age: 1–2[2–3] years approximately

Width around hat: 42[46]cm (16½[18]in)

Hat depth: 16[17]cm (6¼[6¾]in)

Note: Figures in square brackets [ ] refer to larger size; where there is only one set of figures, it applies to both sizes

How much yarn:

1 x 50g (1¾oz) ball of Sirdar Snuggly DK in each of two colours: A – White (shade 251) and B – Black (shade 312)

Hook:

4.00mm (UK 8) crochet hook

Tension:

17 sts and 15 rounds measure 10cm (4in) square over htr on 4.00mm (UK 8) hook

IT IS ESSENTIAL TO WORK TO THE STATED TENSION TO ACHIEVE SUCCESS

What you have to do:

Work hat in continuous rounds of half trebles, increasing as directed. Work last round in slip stitch to produce a firm edge. Make separate shaped pieces in half trebles for ears, eye patches and nose. Embroider features on eye patches. Sew on ears, eye patches and nose.

Instructions

Abbreviations:

beg = beginning
ch = chain(s)
cm = centimetre(s)
cont = continue
dc = double crochet
foll = follow(s)(ing)
htr = half treble
inc = increase(s)(ing)
ss = slip stitch
st(s) = stitch(es)

HAT:

With 4.00mm (UK 8) hook and A, make 3ch.

1st round: Work 6htr into 3rd ch from hook. 6 sts.

Do not join rounds, but insert marker to denote beg/end of round.

2nd round: 2htr into each st. 12 sts.

3rd round: (1htr into next st, 2htr into foll st) 6 times. 18 sts.

4th round: (1htr into each of next 2 sts, 2htr into foll st) 6 times. 24 sts.

5th round: (1htr into each of next 3 sts, 2htr into foll st) 6 times. 30 sts.

6th round: (1htr into each of next 4 sts, 2htr into foll st) 6 times. 36 sts.

7th–12th rounds: Cont in this way, inc 6 sts on each round and working one more st between incs. 72 sts.

First size only:

Work 12 rounds straight in htr.

Second size only:
13th round: (1htr into each of next 11 sts, 2htr into foll st) 6 times. 78 sts.
Work 13 rounds straight in htr.
Both sizes:
Last round: Ss into each htr to end, join with a ss into first htr. Fasten off.

EAR: (make 2)
With 4.00mm (UK 8) hook and B, make 3ch.
1st row: Work 4htr into 3rd ch from hook, turn.
2nd row: 2ch (does not count as a st), 2htr into each htr to end, turn. 8 sts.
3rd row: As 2nd row. 16 sts.
4th row: 1ch (does not count as a st), 1dc into each htr to end. Fasten off.

EYE PATCH: (make 2)
With 4.00mm (UK 8) hook and B, make 4ch.
1st round: Work 1htr into 3rd ch from hook, 3htr into last ch, then cont working into opposite side of foundation ch as foll: 1htr into first ch, 3htr into last ch, join with a ss into first htr. 8 sts.
2nd round: 2ch (does not count as a st), (1htr into each of next 2htr, 2htr into each of foll 2htr) twice, join with a ss into 2nd of 2ch. 12 sts.
3rd round: 2ch, (1htr into each of next 3htr, 2htr into each of foll 3htr) twice, join with a ss into 2nd of 2ch. 18 sts.
4th round: 2ch, (1htr into each of next 4htr, 2htr into each of foll 5htr) twice, join with a ss into 2nd of 2ch. 28 sts. Fasten off.

NOSE:
Work as given for Eye patch to completion of 2nd round. Fasten off.

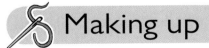 Making up

Flatten hat and sew ears on side fold lines, approximately 9cm (3½in) apart. With B, embroider an eye in each eye patch in satin stitch. With A, sew around outer edge of embroidered eye and sew a small stitch in centre of eye as a highlight. Sew eye patches to front of hat in positions shown. Sew nose centrally to front of hat between eye patches using photograph as a guide to positioning.

Toy horse

Gallop into playtime with this cuddly chestnut pony – he's soft, bendy and easy to look after!

Worked throughout in double crochet, this soft-coloured horse is just the right size to hold or play with and will delight children of all ages.

The Yarn

Patons Diploma Gold DK (approx. 120m/136 yards per 50g/1¾oz ball) contains 55% wool, 25% acrylic and 20% nylon. Machine-washable, it combines wool's good looks with the practical qualities of man-made fibres. There are plenty of colours to choose from, for a realistic-looking horse or a more fantasy-like creature.

GETTING STARTED

★★ Concentration required for shaping and attention to detail for a professional finish.

Size:
Approximately 20cm (8in) high x 24cm (9½in) nose to tail

How much yarn:
1 x 50g (1¾oz) ball of Patons Diploma Gold DK in colour A – Gold (shade 06228)
Oddments in each of colours B – Rust (shade 06211) and C – Black (shade 06183)

Additional items:
Washable polyester toy filling
2 small buttons for eyes
4 craft pipe cleaners (optional)

Hook:
3.50mm (UK 9) crochet hook

Tension:
20 sts and 24 rows measure 10cm (4in) square over dc on 3.50mm (UK 9) hook
IT IS ESSENTIAL TO WORK TO THE STATED TENSION TO ACHIEVE SUCCESS

What you have to do:
Starting at the nose, work the head and body in one piece, working in rounds of double crochet. Make the legs and ears as separate pieces. Use polyester filling to stuff pieces firmly before sewing legs on to body. Attach strands of yarn for mane and tail and plait together.

 Instructions

Abbreviations:

ch = chain(s); **cm** = centimetre(s)
cont = continue; **dc** = double crochet
dc2tog = insert hook into next st, yrh and draw a loop through, insert hook into foll st, yrh and draw a loop through, yrh and draw through all 3 loops
foll = follow(s)(ing); **rem** = remaining
rep = repeat; **RS** = right side; **ss** = slip stitch
st(s) = stitch(es); **WS** = wrong side
yrh = yarn round hook

HEAD AND BODY:
Shape nose:
With 3.50mm (UK 9) hook and C, make 2ch.
1st round: 9dc into 2nd ch from hook, join with a ss in first dc, turn.
2nd round: 1ch, 1dc in each dc to end, join with a ss in first dc, turn.
3rd round: 1ch, 2dc in first dc, (1dc in each of next 2dc, 3dc in next dc) twice, 1dc in each of next 2dc, 1dc in same dc as first 2dc, join with a ss in first dc, turn. 15 sts.

6th row: 1ch, miss first dc, 1dc in each of next 14dc, turn.

7th row: 1ch, miss first dc, 1dc in each of next 12dc, turn.

8th row: 1ch, miss first dc, 1dc in each of next 10dc, turn.

9th row: 1ch, miss first dc, 1dc in each of next 8dc, turn.

10th row: 1ch, miss first dc, 1dc in each of next 6dc, turn.

11th and 12th rows: 1ch, 1dc in each dc to end, turn. 6 sts.

13th row: 1ch, 2dc in first dc, 1dc in next dc, 2dc in each of next 2dc, 1dc in next dc, 2dc in last dc, turn. 10 sts.

14th row: 1ch, 1dc in each st to end, turn.

15th row: 1ch, 2dc in first dc, 1dc in each of next 3dc, 2dc in each of foll 2dc, 1dc in each of next 3dc, 2dc in last dc, turn. 14 sts.

16th row: As 14th row.

17th row: 1ch, 2dc in first dc, 1dc in each of next 5dc, 2dc in each of foll 2dc, 1dc in each of next 5dc, 2dc in last dc, turn. 18 sts.

18th row: As 14th row.

19th row: 1ch, 2dc in first dc, 1dc in each of next 7dc, 2dc in each of foll 2dc, 1dc in each of next 7dc, 2dc in last dc, turn. (These 22 sts form back neck.)

20th row: As 14th row. Fasten off.

With RS facing, rejoin A in centre front under neck st.

Joining round: (RS) 1ch, 1dc in same place as join, 1dc in each of next 3dc across front neck, 1dc in corner, 1dc

4th round: 1ch, 1dc in each dc to end, join with a ss in first dc, turn.

5th round: 1ch, 1dc in each of first 5dc, (4dc in next dc, 1dc in each of next 4dc) twice, join with a ss in first dc, turn. 21 sts.

Change to A.

6th round: 1ch, 1dc in each dc to end, join with a ss in first dc, turn.

Rep last round 8 times more.

Shape head:

1st round: (WS) 1ch, 1dc in each of first 8dc, 2dc in each of next 6dc, 1dc in each of last 7dc, join with a ss in first dc, turn.

2nd round: 1ch, 1dc in each dc to end, join with a ss in first dc, turn.

3rd round: 1ch, 1dc in each of first 12dc, 2dc in each of next 4dc, 1dc in each of last 11dc, join with a ss in first dc, turn. 31 sts.

4th round: As 2nd round. Fasten off.

With RS facing, rejoin A to 4th st of last round.

Shape neck:

**1st row: With RS facing, 1ch, 1dc in each of next 24dc, turn.

2nd row: 1ch, miss first dc, 1dc in each of next 22dc, turn.

3rd row: 1ch, miss first dc, 1dc in each of next 20dc, turn.

4th row: 1ch, miss first dc, 1dc in each of next 18dc, turn.

5th row: 1ch, miss first dc, 1dc in each of next 16dc, turn.

in each of next 22dc around back neck, 1dc in front neck corner, 1dc in each of last 3dc across front neck, join with a ss in first dc, turn. 31 sts**.

Next round: 1ch, 1dc in each st to end, turn.
Rep last round once more.

Next round: 1ch, 1dc in each of next 14dc, 2dc in next dc, 1dc in each of next 14dc, dc2tog, join with a ss in first dc. 31 sts. Fasten off.

Shape chest:
With WS facing, count back 12 sts from end of last round and rejoin yarn in this st. Work as given for neck from **
to **, joining in at centre back neck before working joining round and reading back for front on joining round. Fasten off.

Shape body:
Rejoin yarn at underside of body so that joins will be under horse.

Next round: 1ch, 1dc in each st to end, join with a ss in first dc, turn.
Rep last round 19 times more.

Shape bottom:
1st round: 1ch, 1dc in first dc, (dc2tog) twice, 1dc in each dc to last 4dc, (dc2tog) twice, join with a ss in first dc. 27 sts.

2nd round: 1ch, 1dc in each st to end, join with a ss in first dc, turn.

3rd round: 1ch, 1dc in first dc, (dc2tog, 1dc in next dc) 8 times, dc2tog, join with a ss in first dc, turn. 18 sts.

4th round: As 2nd round, but do not turn at end.

5th round: 1ch, (dc2tog) 9 times, join with a ss in first dc. 9 sts. Fasten off, leaving a long end.

LEGS: (make 4)
With 3.50mm (UK 9) hook and C, make 2ch.
Working in rounds with RS of work facing throughout, cont as foll:

1st round: 8dc in 2nd ch from hook, join with a ss in first dc. 8 sts.

2nd round: 1ch, 2dc in each of first 4dc, 1dc in each of last 4dc, join with a ss in first dc. 12 sts.

3rd round: 1ch, 1dc in each dc, join with a ss in first dc.
Rep last round once more.
Change to A and rep 3rd round 16 times more.
Fasten off.

EARS: (make 2)
With 3.50mm (UK 9) hook and A, make 4ch.

1st row: 1dc in 2nd ch from hook, 1dc in each st to end, turn. 3 sts.

2nd row: 1ch, 2dc in first dc, 1dc in next st, 2dc in last dc, turn.

3rd row: 1ch, 2dc in first dc, 1dc in each of next 3 sts, 2dc in last dc, turn. 7 sts.

4th row: 1dc, 1dc in each st to end.
Rep last row twice more.

Next row: 1ch, dc2tog, 1dc in each of next 3 sts, dc2tog, turn.

Next row: 1ch, dc2tog, 1dc in next st, dc2tog, turn.

Next row: 1ch, 1dc in next st, dc2tog.
Fasten off.

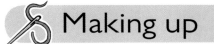

Making up

Thread long end left at last round of body through sts, pull up tightly and secure. Fold first 2 rounds at nose inwards and pinch sides together. Stitch in a cross shape to form mouth. Join neck seams and one side of chest seam. Stuff head and body firmly with toy filling and join rem chest seam. Sew an eye to each side of head, passing thread through head several times to secure. Sew ears close together on top of head just above eyes. Stuff legs firmly and sew to body. If desired, cut craft pipe cleaners to same length as legs and insert one into each leg before sewing to body.

Mane:
Cut 6 lengths of B each 30cm (12in) long. Thread through centre back neck just behind ears and pull up to same length. Cut another 6 lengths of B to same length and thread singly through every 2 rows down centre back neck. Divide top bunch of threads into 3 groups of 4 and start to plait them, incorporating single lengths as you come to them to form a French braid. Secure with a knot and trim ends.

Forelock:
With B, make a small tassel and stitch in place at the top of mane between ears.

Tail:
Cut 6 lengths of B each 25cm (10in) long. Find centre and sew this point securely to rear of horse. Divide into 3 groups of 4 and plait ends for 8cm (3in). Secure with a knot and trim ends.

Child's ballerina cardigan

A classic crossover ballerina-style cardigan for a special aspiring dancer.

Worked in a soft double knitting yarn, this sweet flower-embroidered cardigan with crossover fronts and ties is a popular style for little girls.

The Yarn

Orkney Angora St Magnus 50/50 DK (approx. 400m/ 436 yards per 100g/3½oz ball) is a blend of 50% angora with 50% lambswool. It is a soft, versatile hand-dyed yarn and there are 35 beautiful colours to choose from.

GETTING STARTED

★★ Stitch pattern and shaping require concentration.

Size:
To fit chest: 56[61:66]cm (22[24:26]in)
Actual size: 56[61:66]cm (22[24:26]in)
Length to shoulder: 30.5[34:37.5]cm (12[13½:14¾]in)
Sleeve seam: 21.5[26.5:29]cm (8½[10¼:11½]in)
Note: Figures in square brackets [ ] refer to larger sizes; where there is only one set of figures, it applies to all sizes
How much yarn:
4[4:5] x 50g (1¾oz) balls of Orkney Angora St Magnus 50/50 DK in colour A – Cerise (shade 21)
1 ball in each of colours B – Burgundy (shade 2) and C – Magenta (shade 20)
Hooks:
3.00mm (UK 10) crochet hook, 4.00mm (UK 8) crochet hook
Tension:
7.5 gps and 18 rows measure 10cm (4in) square over patt on 4.00mm (UK 8) hook
IT IS ESSENTIAL TO WORK TO THE STATED TENSION TO ACHIEVE SUCCESS
What you have to do:
Work main fabric in stitch pattern as described. Use shaping as described for armholes, back neck, front slopes and sleeves. Neaten outer edges with double crochet and chain loop border. Embroider lazy daisy flowers on to finished cardigan.

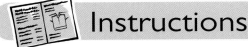 ## Instructions

Abbreviations:

beg = beginning; **ch** = chain(s); **cm** = centimetre(s); **cont** = continue(s); **dc** = double crochet; **dec** = decrease(d); **foll** = follow(s)(ing); **gp(s)** = group(s) consisting of 1dc, 1ch and 1tr; **inc** = increase(d); **patt** = pattern; **rep** = repeat; **RS** = right side; **sp(s)** = space(s); **ss** = slip stitch; **st** = stitch; **tog** = together; **tr** = treble(s); **WS** = wrong side; **2dc tog** = work 1dc in each of next 2 sts leaving last loop of each on hook, yarn round hook and draw through all 3 loops

BACK:

With 4.00mm (UK 8) hook and A, make 67[73:79]ch.
Foundation row: (RS) 1tr in 4th ch from hook, *miss 2ch, 1 gp in next ch, rep from * to last 3ch, miss 2ch, 1dc in last ch, turn. 21[23:25] gps.
Patt row: 3ch, 1tr in first dc, *miss 1tr and 1ch, 1gp in next dc, rep from * ending with miss last tr, 1dc in 2nd of 3ch, turn.
Rep patt row until Back measures 18.5[21:23.5]cm (7¼[8¼:9¼]in) from beg, ending with a WS row.

Shape armholes:

1st dec row: Ss across (1dc, 1tr, 1ch, 1dc), 2ch, 1tr in same dc, patt as set, ending with 1dc in last dc, turn leaving 1tr and 3ch unworked.

2nd dec row: 2ch, 1tr in first dc, patt as set, ending with 2dc tog over last dc and foll tr, turn.

3rd dec row: Patt as set, ending with 2dc tog over last dc and foll tr. 2 gps dec at each side – 17[19:21] gps. Cont in patt until Back measures 28.5[32:35.5]cm (11½[12½:14]in) from beg, ending with a WS row.

Shape back neck:

Next row: 3ch, 1tr in first dc, patt 4[5:5] gps, miss 1tr and 1ch, 1dc in next dc, turn and complete this side of neck first.

Next row: Ss in first tr, 2ch, miss 1ch, patt to end. Fasten off. With RS of work facing, miss 6[6:8] gps at centre back neck and rejoin yarn to dc of next gp.

Next row: 2ch, 1tr in same dc, miss 1tr and 1ch, patt 4[5:5] gps, miss 1tr, 1dc in 2nd of 3ch, turn.

Next row: 3ch, 1tr in first dc, patt 3[4:4] gps, miss 1tr and 1ch, 1dc in next dc. Fasten off.

RIGHT FRONT:

With 4.00mm (UK 8) hook and A, make 52[58:64]ch. Work foundation row and patt row as given for Back. 16[18:20] gps. Rep patt row until Right front measures 18 rows less than Back to armhole shaping, ending with a WS row.**

Shape front edge:

1st dec row: 2ch, 1tr in first dc, patt to end, turn.

2nd dec row: Patt as set, ending with 1dc in last dc, 1ch,

1dc in last tr, turn.

3rd dec row: 2ch, miss 1dc and 1ch, 1 gp in next dc, patt to end, turn.

4th dec row: Patt as set, ending with 1dc in last dc, turn.

5th dec row: As 1st dec row.

6th dec row: Patt as set, ending with 2dc tog over last dc and foll tr, turn. 2 gps dec at front edge – 14[16:18] gps. Rep these 6 rows twice more (Right front now matches Back to armhole shaping).

Shape armhole:

Cont to shape front edge AT SAME TIME shape armhole as foll:

Next row: 2ch, 1tr in first dc, patt as set, ending with 1dc in last dc, turn (leaving 1tr and 3ch unworked).

Next row: 2ch, 1tr in first dc, patt as set, ending with 1dc in last dc, 1ch, 1dc in last tr, turn.

Next row: 2ch, miss 1dc and 1ch, 1 gp in next dc, patt as set, ending with 2dc tog over last dc and foll tr, turn. 2 gps dec at armhole edge.

Cont to dec at front edge as set until 4[5:5] gps rem. Work straight until Right front measures same as Back to shoulder, ending with a WS row. Fasten off.

LEFT FRONT:

Work as given for Right front to **.

Shape front edge:

1st dec row: Patt as set, ending with 1dc in last dc, 1ch, miss last tr, 1dc in top of 3ch, turn.

2nd dec row: 2ch, miss 1dc and 1ch, 1 gp in next dc, patt to end, turn.

3rd dec row: Patt as set, ending with 1dc in last dc, turn.

4th dec row: 2ch, 1tr in first dc, patt to end, turn.

5th dec row: Patt as set, ending with 2dc tog over last dc and foll tr, turn.

6th dec row: 3ch, 1tr in first st, patt to end. 2 gps dec at front edge – 14[16:18] gps. Rep these 6 rows twice more (Left front now matches Back to armhole shaping).

Shape armhole:

Cont to shape front edge AT SAME TIME shape armhole as foll:

Next row: Ss across (1tr, 1ch and 1dc), 2ch, 1tr in same dc patt as set ending with 1dc in last dc, 1ch, miss last tr, 1dc in top of 3ch, turn.

Next row: 2ch, miss 1dc and 1ch, 1 gp in next dc, patt as set, ending with 2dc tog over last dc and foll tr, turn.

Next row: Patt as set, ending with 1dc in last dc, turn. 2 gps dec at armhole edge.

Cont to dec at front edge as set until 4[5:5] gps rem. Work straight until Left front measures same as Back to shoulder, ending with a WS row. Fasten off.

SLEEVES: (make 2)

With 4.00mm (UK 8) hook and A, make 40[40:46]ch. Work foundation row and patt row as given for Back. 12[12:14] gps. Rep patt row until Sleeve measures 6.5cm (2½in) from beg, ending with a WS row.

Shape sleeve:

1st inc row: Patt as set, ending with 1dc and 1tr in 2nd of 3ch, turn.

2nd inc row: 2ch, miss first tr, 1 gp in first dc, patt as set, ending with 1dc and 1tr in 2nd of 3ch, turn.

3rd inc row: 2ch, miss first tr, 1 gp in first dc, patt as set, ending with 1dc in last dc, 1tr in next ch, turn.

4th and 5th inc rows: As 3rd inc row.

6th inc row: 3ch, 1tr in first tr, 1 gp in next dc, patt as set, ending with 1 gp in last dc, 1dc in next ch, turn.

7th and 8th inc rows: Patt as set. (1 gp inc at each side) Rep these 8 rows 2[3:3] times more. 18[20:22] gps. Work straight until Sleeve measures 20.5[25.5:28]cm (8[10:11]in) from beg, ending with a WS row.

Shape sleeve top:

1st dec row: Ss across (1dc, 1tr, 1ch and 1dc), 2ch, 1tr in same dc, patt as set, ending with 1dc in last dc, turn leaving 1tr and 3ch unworked.

2nd dec row: 2ch, 1tr in dc at base of these 2ch, patt as set, ending with 2dc tog over last dc and foll tr, turn. Rep last row 6 times more. 5 gps dec at either side.

Last row: Miss 2dc tog, ss across 1tr, 1ch and 1dc, 1ch,

1dc in next tr, patt as set to last 3 gps, 2dc tog over next dc and foll tr. Fasten off.

Making up

Press according to directions on ball band. Join shoulder seams, matching patts. Sew in sleeve tops, then join side and sleeve seams.

Cuffs:

With 3.00mm (UK 10) hook, B and RS of work facing, join in yarn at sleeve seam.

1st round: 1ch, 1dc in base of each ch all around, ending 1ss in 1ch at beg of round.

2nd round: *3ch, miss 1dc, 1ss in next dc, rep from * ending 1ss in same place as base of first 3ch of round. Fasten off.

Front, neck and lower border:

With 3.00mm (UK 10) hook, B and RS of work facing, join in yarn at one side seam.

1st round: 1ch, 1dc in base of each ch of lower edge to corner, 3dc in same place at corner, 5dc in side edge of every 4 rows to beg of front shaping, 2dc in same place at this corner, 5dc in side edge of every 4 rows to back neck corner, 2dc tog at this corner, then cont all around in this way, ending 1ss in 1ch at beg of round.

2nd round: As 2nd round of Cuffs, but at each outward corner work 3ch, ss in next dc. Fasten off.

Ties: (make 2)

With 3.00mm (UK 10) hook and B, make 5ch.

1st row: 1dc in 2nd ch from hook, 1dc in each of next 3ch, turn.

2nd row: 1ch, 1dc in each of 4dc, turn. Rep last row until Tie measures 27.5[30:32.5]cm (10¾[11¾:12¾]in). Fasten off. Sew one tie to Right front edge behind border, just below beg of front shaping. Sew other Tie in corresponding position on Left side seam.

Embroidery:

With tapestry needle and C, work flowers consisting of 6 lazy daisy sts (equal-length straight sts radiating from a central point) arranged around a hole in the crochet patt at random using photograph as a guide.

Heirloom baby bootees

Fine yarn and the pretty tiny motif make these bootees miniature works of art.

Make these charming shoes as a gift for a baby. Worked in a fine cotton yarn and mainly in trebles, they will be treasured for years to come.

GETTING STARTED

⭐ ⭐ *Straightforward stitches but worked in a very fine yarn*

Size:
To fit baby 6–9 months
Finished bootees measure 10.5cm (4⅛) in long

How much yarn:
1 x 50g (1¾oz) ball of Twilleys Lyscordet in
A – White (shade 78)
1 skein of DMC No.5 Perle Cotton in each of B – Variegated Pink (shade 4180) and C – Variegated Green (shade 4050)

Hook:
2.00mm (UK 14) crochet hook

Additional items:
3cm (1¼in) length of 2cm- (¾in-) wide Velcro
2 x 1cm (½in) buttons
White sewing cotton and needle

Tension:
30 sts and 16 rows measure 10cm (4in) square in Lyscordet on 2.00mm (UK 14) hook
IT IS ESSENTIAL TO WORK TO THE STATED TENSION TO ACHIEVE SUCCESS

What you have to do:
Work bootee in rounds of trebles, shaping as directed. Work top edging in contrast thread and double crochet. Make separate flower and leaf motifs in variegated threads and sew onto bootee. Sew on fastening topped with decorative button.

The Yarn

Twilleys Lyscordet (approx. 200m/218 yards per 50g/ 1¾oz ball) is 100% mercerised fine cotton yarn, popular for finer crochet work. As well as white, it is available in a range of colours. DMC No. 5 Perle Cotton (approx. 25m/27 yards per skein) is 100% mercerised cotton with a twisted, lustruous finish, suitable for both embroidery and crochet. There is a large colour range.

Instructions

Abbreviations:

ch = chain
cm = centimetre(s)
cont = continue
dc = double crochet
dtr = double treble
foll = follows
htr = half treble
rep = repeat
RS = right side
ss = slip stitch
st(s) = stitch(es)
tr = treble
tr2tog = work 1tr into each of next 2 sts, leaving last loop of each on hook, yarn round hook and draw through all 3 loops

Note:
The buttons are a decorative option as the bootees are fastened with Velcro.

BOOTEE: (make 2)
Sole:
With 2.00mm (UK 14) hook and A, make 20ch. Cont in rounds as foll:

1st round: 5tr into 4th ch from hook, 1tr into each of next 15ch, 6tr into last ch, then cont along other side of foundation ch as foll: 1tr into each of next 15ch, join with a ss into 3rd of 3ch. 42 sts.

2nd round: 3ch (counts as first tr), 1tr into st at base of ch, 2tr into each of next 5 sts, 1tr into each of next 15 sts, 2tr into each of next 6 sts, 1tr into each of next 15 sts, join with a ss into 3rd of 3ch. 54 sts.

3rd round: 3ch, 1tr into st at base of ch, 2tr into each of next 11 sts, 1tr into each of next 16 sts, (2tr into next st, 1tr into next st) twice, 1tr into each of next 3 sts, (2tr into next st, 1tr into next st) twice, 1tr into each of next 15 sts, join with a ss into 3rd of 3ch. 70 sts.

4th round: 3ch, 1tr into next tr, (2tr into next st, 1tr into next st) 10 times, 1tr into each of next 20 sts, (2tr into next st, 1tr into next st) twice, 1tr into each of next 3 sts, (2tr into next st, 1tr into next st) twice, 1tr into each of next 17 sts, join with a ss into 3rd of 3ch. 84 sts.

Sides:

5th and 6th rounds: 3ch, 1tr into each st to end, join with a ss into 3rd of 3ch.

7th round: 3ch, (tr2tog over next 2 sts) 24 times, tr2tog over next 2 sts and mark this st for ankle strap, tr2tog over next 2 sts, 1tr into each of next 11 sts, (tr2tog over next 2 sts) 10 times, join with a ss into 3rd of 3ch.

Toe:

1st row: 3ch, miss st at base of ch, (tr2tog over next 2 sts) 8 times, turn.

2nd row: 3ch, miss st at base of ch, (tr2tog over next 2 sts) 4 times, turn.

Next round: 2ch (counts as first htr), miss st at base of ch, 1htr into each of next 4 sts, 2htr into first row end, 1htr into next row end, 1htr into each st, 1htr into next row end, 2htr into last row end, join with a ss into 2nd of 2ch. Fasten off.

Ankle strap:

Last row: Rejoin yarn in st above marker, make 19ch for strap, 1tr into 4th ch from hook, 1tr into each of next 15ch, 1tr into same st as rejoined yarn, 1tr into each of next 14 sts around back of bootee, make 19ch for strap, 1tr into 4ch from hook, 1tr into each of next 15ch, ss into st at base of next tr. Fasten off.

Edging:

With 2.00mm (UK 14) hook and RS of work facing, join B to st where yarn was joined for ankle strap, 1ch, 1dc into each st along strap, 2dc into end of strap, 1dc into each st along top of strap, 2dc into end of strap, 1dc into each st along other side of strap and around top of bootee, ss into 1ch. Fasten off.

MOTIF:

Flower:

1st round: Wind B 10 times around end of a pencil, slide off loop and, with 2.00mm (UK 14) hook, work 2ch, 13dc into loop, join with a ss into 2nd of 2ch.

2nd round: *(1htr, 1tr, 1dtr, 1tr and 1htr) all into next st, ss into next st, rep from * to end. Fasten off.

Leaves:

With 2.00mm (UK 14) hook and C, *make 7ch, 1dc into 2nd ch from hook, 1tr into next ch, 1dtr into each of next 3ch, 1tr into last ch, rep from * twice more. Fasten off.

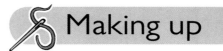

Making up

Sew leaves to back of flower, then sew flower to front of bootee as shown in the photograph. Sew a button to end of one strap. Cut a 1 x 2cm (½ x ¾in) strip of Velcro and trim ends to same curve as strap. Slip stitch fluffy piece to back of strap with button and hooked piece to front of other strap. Make up second bootee in same way, reversing fastening for strap.

Angel fish cushion

Crochet your child a fishy friend in the form of this bold striped cushion to give their room an underwater theme.

Children will love this fun tropical fish cushion in bright stripes. The body is worked in easy stitches, while the lightly padded fins feature a pretty shell pattern.

The Yarn

Debbie Bliss Eco Aran (approx. 90m/98 yards per 50g/1¾oz ball) contains 100% organic cotton in an aran weight. It is produced by means of an ecological and socially conscious process without the use of harmful chemicals. The colour palette has a good range of neutral shades as well as bright ones.

GETTING STARTED

★★ *Basic stitches, but plenty of shaping to concentrate on.*

Size:

Length from nose to tail: approximately 61cm (24in)
Height: approximately 40cm (15¾in)

How much yarn:

3 x 50g (1¾oz) balls of Debbie Bliss Eco Aran in colour A – Orange (shade 601)
2 balls in colour B – White (shade 608)
1 ball in colour C – Black (shade 618)

Hook:

4.50mm (UK 7) crochet hook

Additional items:

40cm (15¾in) square cushion pad
Washable polyester toy filling
15cm (6in) square of polyester wadding

Tension:

15 sts and 10 rows measure 10cm (4in) square over patt on 4.50mm (UK 7) hook
IT IS ESSENTIAL TO WORK TO THE STATED TENSION TO ACHIEVE SUCCESS

What you have to do:

Work front and back in half trebles and trebles, working in stripes and shaping as directed. Work eyes in the round. Make separate fins in shell pattern. Insert wadding into folded fins and sew them into cushion seams when joining front and back. Insert stuffing into nose of cushion before adding cushion pad.

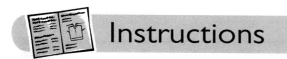

Instructions

Abbreviations:

ch = chain(s)
cm = centimetre(s)
cont = continue
dc = double crochet
foll = follows
htr = half treble
htr2tog = yrh, insert hook into back loop only of next st and draw through a loop, yrh and draw through first 2 loops on hook, yrh, insert hook into front loop only of next st, yrh and draw through a loop, yrh and draw through all 4 loops
inc = increase
patt = pattern
rem = remain
rep = repeat
RS = right side
sp(s) = space(s)
ss = slip stitch
st(s) = stitch(es)
tr = treble
yrh = yarn round hook

FRONT BODY:

With 4.50mm (UK 7) hook and A, make 4ch.

1st row: 1htr into 3rd ch from hook, 1htr into last ch, turn. 3 sts.

2nd row: 2ch (counts as first htr), 1htr into back loop only of st at base of ch, 1htr into back loop only of next st, 2htr into front loop only of 2nd of 2ch, turn. 5 sts.

3rd row: 2ch, 1htr into back loop only of st at base of ch, 1htr into back loop only of each st, ending with 2htr into front loop only of 2nd of 2ch, turn. 7 sts.

4th–6th rows: As 3rd row. 13 sts.
Cont in patt as set and inc one st at each end of every row, working in stripes as foll: 1 row C; 6 rows B; 1 row C; 12 rows A; 1 row C and 2 rows B. 59 sts.

Next row: With B, 2ch (counts as first htr), miss st at base of ch, 1htr into back loop only of each st, 1htr into front loop of 2nd of 2ch, turn.

Next row: With C, 2ch, miss st at base of ch, miss next st, 1htr into back loop only of each st to last 2 sts, htr2tog over next st and top of turning ch, turn. 57 sts. Rep last row 21 times more, working in stripes as foll:

2 rows B; 1 row C; 12 rows A; 1 row C and 5 rows B.

Next row: With B, 2ch, miss st at base of ch, miss next st, 1htr into back loop only of each st to end, 2htr into 2nd of 2ch, turn. 15 sts. Change to C and rep last row.

Shape tail:

Cont in C only.

1st row: 3ch (counts as first tr), miss st at base of ch, 1tr into each of next 6 sts, 2ch, 1tr into next st, 2ch, 1tr into each st to end, working last tr into turning ch, turn.

2nd row: 3ch, miss st at base of ch, 1tr into each of next 6tr, (1tr, 2ch and 1tr) into next 2ch sp, 2ch, (1tr, 2ch and 1tr) into next 2ch sp, 1tr into each tr to end, working last tr into 3rd of 3ch, turn.

3rd row: 3ch, miss st at base of ch, 1tr into each of next 7tr, *(1tr, 2ch and 1tr) into next 2ch sp, 2ch, rep from * once more, (1tr, 2ch and 1tr) into next 2ch sp, 1tr into each tr to end, working last tr into 3rd of 3ch, turn.

4th row: 3ch, miss st at base of ch, 1tr into each of next 8tr, (1tr, 2ch and 1tr) into each of next five 2ch sps, 1tr into each tr to end, working last tr into 3rd of 3ch, turn.

5th row: 3ch, miss st at base of ch, 1tr into each tr and 2tr into each 2ch sp to end, working last tr into 3rd of 3ch. Fasten off.

BACK BODY:

Work as given for Front Body.

EYES: (make 2)

With 4.50mm (UK 7) hook and B, make 2ch.

1st round: 8dc into 2nd ch from hook, join with a ss into first dc. 8 sts.
Change to C.
2nd round: 2ch, 2htr into each st to end, join with a ss into first htr. 16 sts.
3rd round: 2ch, *1htr into next st, 2htr into next st, rep from * to end, join with a ss into first htr. 24 sts. Fasten off.

FINS: (make 2)
With 4.50mm (UK 7) hook and A, make 26ch.
Foundation row: 1dc into 2nd ch from hook, *miss 2ch, 5tr into next ch, miss 2ch, 1dc into next ch, rep from * to end, turn.
1st row: 3ch (counts as first tr), 2tr into st at base of ch, *miss 2tr, 1dc into next tr, miss 2tr, 5tr into next dc, rep from *, ending with 3tr into last dc, turn.
2nd row: 1ch, 1dc into st at base of ch, *miss 2tr, 5tr into next dc, miss 2tr, 1dc into next tr, rep from *, ending with 1dc into 3rd of 3ch, turn.
Rep last 2 rows 5 times more. Fasten off.

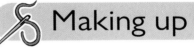 ## Making up

Using picture as a guide, sew eyes in position to front and back. Cut square of wadding in half diagonally. Fold fins in half diagonally over piece of wadding and oversew open edges together. Pin one oversewn fin edge in place to upper and lower back edges of one body piece, with folded edge uppermost.
Place front and back body pieces together with RS facing and stitch together along upper and lower back edges of fish, enclosing fins in seam and leaving tail open. Now stitch upper front edge of fish closed and section in A on nose at lower front edge.
Turn RS out. Backstitch through both layers at start of tail and then oversew around outer tail edges. Insert a little toy stuffing into nose of fish and then insert cushion pad. Stitch opening closed at lower front edge.

Star decorations

These starry motifs in jewel-bright colours can be used individually or joined into a garland.

These colourful decorations, based on six colours and a variety of stripe combinations, feature a circular motif worked in double and treble crochet with a star-pointed edging.

The Yarn

Anchor Style Creativa Fino (approx. 125m/136 yards per 50g/1¾oz) contains 100% mercerized cotton. This crisp 4 ply yarn is ideal for craft projects, especially as the range contains plenty of fabulous colours.

GETTING STARTED

Each decoration comprises two easy circular motifs with joining and edging rounds.

Size:

Decorations measure approximately 9cm (3½in) in diameter

How much yarn:

1 x 50g (1¾oz) ball of Anchor Style Creativa Fino in each of six colours – Yellow (shade 01326); Blue (shade 01323); Orange (shade 01338); Pink (shade 01320); Green (shade 00253) and Red (shade 01318)

Hook:

2.50mm (UK 12) crochet hook

Tension:

First 3 rounds of circular motif measure 4.5cm (1¾in) in diameter on 2.50mm (UK 12) hook

IT IS ESSENTIAL TO WORK TO THE STATED TENSION TO ACHIEVE SUCCESS

What you have to do:

For each decoration, make two circular motifs with each round in a different colour. Use fifth colour to join motifs together around the outer edge with a round of star points incorporating a hanging loop.

![book icon] # Instructions

Abbreviations:

ch = chain(s)
cm = centimetre(s)
dc = double crochet
dtr = double treble
foll = follows
htr = half treble
rep = repeat
RS = right side
ss = slip stitch
st(s) = stitch(es)
tr = treble
WS = wrong side

Note: We made 12 decorations, varying the sequence of colours on each one. When changing colour, always introduce new colour on last part of last st in previous colour.

STAR DECORATION:

Circle: (make 2)

With 2.50mm (UK 12) hook and 1st colour, make a magic circle (see Note on page 66).

1st round: 1ch (does not count as a st), work 8dc into ring, change to 2nd colour to join with a ss into first dc, 8 sts. Pull end of yarn up tightly to close circle.

2nd round: 3ch, 1tr into st at base

of ch, 2tr into each st to end, change to 3rd colour to join with a ss into 3rd of 3ch. 16 sts.

3rd round: As 2nd round, changing to 4th colour at end of round. 32 sts.

4th round: 3ch, miss st at base of ch, (2tr into next st, 1tr into next st) to last st, 2tr into last st, join with a ss into 3rd of 3ch. 48 sts. Fasten off.

Place two circles with WS together (ends do not need to be woven in as they will be hidden between the two layers and help to pad out centre of decoration) and join as foll:

Joining round: With RS of work facing, join 5th colour to any st on last round, 4ch, working into back loop only of each pair of corresponding sts all around circle, work 1tr into st at base of ch, 1htr into next st, 1dc into next st, ss into each of next 2 sts, *1dc into next st, 1htr into next st, 1tr and 1dtr into next st, 3ch, ss into top of dtr, 1dtr and 1tr into next st, 1htr into next st, 1dc into next st, ss into each of next 2 sts, rep from * 4 more times, 1dc into next st, 1htr into next st, 1tr and 1dtr into last st, 16ch, join with a ss into 4th of 4ch. Fasten off.

Bouclé baby jacket

This yarn is so soft that the lucky baby wearing it will definitely be extra cuddly.

With its rounded collar and buttoned fronts, this baby jacket is worked in a chunky bouclé yarn to resemble fur – but it is easily washable.

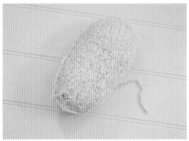

The Yarn
King Cole Cuddles Chunky (approx. 125m/ 136 yards per 50g/1¾oz ball) is 100% polyester. It is soft and textured with a fur-like appearance. Available in pale baby colours, this practical yarn is machine-washable.

GETTING STARTED

★★ *Very easy stitches, but working textured yarn requires patience.*

Size:
To fit age: *6–9[9–12:12–18] months*
To fit chest: *43[45.5:48]cm (17[18:19]in)*
Actual size: *54[58:66]cm (21¼[22¾:26]in)*
Length: *25[29:33]cm (9¾[11½:13]in)*
Sleeve seam: *13.5[16.5:18.5]cm (5¼[6½:7¼]in)*
Note: *Figures in square brackets [ ] refer to larger sizes; where there is only one set of figures, it applies to all sizes*

How much yarn:
2[3:3] x 50g (1¾oz) balls of King Cole Cuddles Chunky in Sky (shade 352)

Hook:
7.00mm (UK 2) crochet hook
Additional items:
3 buttons
Tension:
10 sts and 9 rows measure 10cm (4in) square over htr on 7.00mm (UK 2) hook
IT IS ESSENTIAL TO WORK TO THE STATED TENSION TO ACHIEVE SUCCESS
What you have to do:
Work throughout in half trebles. Shape armholes, neck and sleeves as instructed. Make buttonholes in right front edge for a girl or left front edge for a boy.

Instructions

Abbreviations:

alt = alternate
beg = beginning
ch = chain(s)
cm = centimetre(s)
cont = continue
htr = half treble
htr2tog = (yrh, insert hook in next st, yrh and draw a loop through) twice, yrh and draw through all 5 loops on hook
inc = increase(d)
patt = pattern
rep = repeat
st(s) = stitch(es)
yrh = yarn round hook

BACK:

With 7.00mm (UK 2) hook make 28[30:34]ch fairly loosely.

Foundation row: 1htr into 3rd ch from hook, 1htr into each ch to end, turn. 27[29:33] sts.

Patt row: 2ch (counts as first htr), miss st at base of ch, 1htr into each st to end, working last htr into 2nd of 2ch, turn. Patt 9[11:13] rows more.

Shape armholes:

Next row: 2ch (does NOT count as a st), htr2tog over next 2 sts, patt to last 3 sts, htr2tog over next 2 sts, turn leaving 2ch unworked. 23[25:29] sts.
Patt 9[11:13] rows more.

Shape shoulders and back neck:

Next row: 2ch, patt 7[8:9] sts, turn and complete this side of neck first.

Next row: 2ch, miss st at base of ch, htr2tog over next 2 sts, patt 2[2:3] sts. Fasten off.

Rejoin yarn to beg of last row before shaping shoulders and back neck and

work as given for first side. Leave 7[7:9] sts at centre for back neck.

FIRST FRONT:

(This is Left front for Girl's version or Right front for Boy's version.)
With 7.00mm (UK 2) hook make 16[17:19]ch fairly loosely. Work foundation row as given for Back. 15[16:18] sts.**
Cont in htr, work 10[12:14] rows.

Shape armhole:

Next row: 2ch (does NOT count as a st), htr2tog over next 2 sts, patt to end, turn. 13[14:16] sts.
Patt 7[9:11] rows.

Shape neck:

Next row: Patt 9[10:11] sts, turn.

Next row: 2ch, miss st at base of ch, htr2tog over next 2 sts, patt to end, turn.

Next row: Patt to last 2 sts, htr2tog over last 2 sts, turn.

Next row: Patt 4[4:5] sts. Fasten off.

SECOND FRONT:

(This is Right front for Girl's version or Left front for Boy's version.) Work as given for First front to **.
Patt 7[11:14] rows.

1st and 2nd sizes only:

Next row: (make buttonhole) 2ch, miss st at base of ch, 1htr into next htr, 1ch, miss 1st, patt to end, turn. Patt 2[0] rows.

All sizes:

Shape armhole:

Next row: 2ch (does NOT count as a st), hr2tog over next 2 sts, patt to end, turn. 13[14:16] sts.
Patt 0[2:0] rows.

Next row: (make buttonhole) 2ch, miss st at base of ch, 1htr into next st, 1ch, miss 1st, patt to end, turn. *Patt 3 rows, then work buttonhole on next row. * Rep from * to * 0[0:1] times. Patt 2 rows.

Shape neck:

Work as given for First Front.

SLEEVES: (make 2)

With 7.00mm (UK 2) hook make 15[17:19]ch fairly loosely. Work foundation row as given for Back.
14[16:18] sts.

Next row: 2ch (counts as first htr), 1htr into st at base of ch, 1htr into each st to end, working 2htr into 2nd of 2ch. 1 st inc at each end of row.
Cont in htr, inc 1 st at each end of every foll alt row until

there are 26[30:32] sts.
Work 0[1:3] rows straight.

Shape top:

Next row: 2ch (does NOT count as a st), htr2tog over next 2 sts, patt to last 3 sts, htr2tog over next 2 sts, turn leaving 2ch unworked. 22[26:28] sts.
Patt 1 row. Fasten off.

COLLAR:

Join shoulder seams.
With 7.00mm (UK 2) hook, join yarn to neck edge 2 sts in from right front edge, 2ch (counts as first htr), miss st at base of ch, work 5[5:6]htr evenly up right front neck edge, 11[11:13]htr around back neck and 6[6:7] htr evenly down left front neck, ending 2 sts from front edge, turn. 23[23:27] sts. Patt 3 rows.

Next 2 rows: 2ch, miss st at base of ch, htr2tog over next 2 sts, patt to last 3 sts, htr2tog over next 2 sts, 1htr into 2nd of 2ch, turn. Fasten off.

Making up

Sew sleeves into armholes. Join side and sleeve seams. Sew on buttons to correspond with buttonholes.

Amigurumi animal charms

Children will be delighted to catch onto the craze for amigurumi with these little creatures

Customise key rings, pencil cases and other accessories with this menagerie of cute charms. Worked in double crochet in the round, these appealing pets have stitched-on facial details.

The Yarn
Anchor Style Creativa (approx. 70m/76 yards per 50g/1¾oz ball) is 100% mercerized cotton. It produces a soft and silky fabric with a subtle sheen that is ideal to use for craft projects and there is a good wide range of contemporary colours to choose from.

Instructions

Note: When fastening off each piece, leave a long tail to use for sewing up.

ELEPHANT CHARM:
Head:
With 4.00mm (UK 8) hook and A, make a magic circle (see Note on page 66) as foll: Wind A several times around tip of left forefinger. Carefully slip ring off finger, insert hook into ring, pull yarn through and make 1ch, then work 6dc in ring, join with a ss in first dc. Pull end of yarn gently to close ring. 6 sts.

Marking beg of each round, and noting that 1st–10th rounds are worked with WS facing (RS inside), cont as foll:

1st round: 2dc in each st to end. 12 sts.
2nd round: (2dc in next st, 1dc in next st) to end. 18 sts.
3rd round: 1dc in each st to end.
4th round: (2dc in next st, 1dc in each of next 2 sts) to end. 24 sts.
5th–7th rounds: As 3rd.
8th round: (Dc2tog over next 2 sts, 1dc in each of next 2 sts) to end. 18 sts.

Abbreviations:
beg = beginning
ch = chain(s)
cm = centimetre(s)
cont = continue
dc = double crochet
dc2tog = (insert hook
in next st, yrh and
draw a loop through)
twice, yrh and draw
through all 3 loops
foll = follows
htr = half treble
ss = slip stitch
st(s) = stitch(es)
tr = treble
WS = wrong side
yrh = yarn round hook

9th round: As 3rd.
10th round: (Dc2tog over next 2 sts, 1dc in next st) to end. 12 sts.
Turn work inside out (RS outside). Stuff head firmly with polyester filling. Cont to work with WS facing.
11th round: (Dc2tog over next 2 sts) to end. 6 sts.
12th round: (Dc2tog over next 2 sts) to end.
Fasten off, leaving a long end. Use long end to neaten hole at base of head.

Left ear:
With 4.00mm (UK 8) hook and B, make a magic circle (see Note on page 66) and make 1ch, then work 7dc in ring, join with a ss in first dc. Pull end of yarn gently to close ring. 7 sts.
1st round: 2dc in each st to end. 14 sts.
2nd round: (2dc in next st, 1dc in next st) to end. 21 sts.
3rd round: 1htr in next st, 1tr in each of next 2 sts, 2tr in next st, 1tr in next st, 2tr in next st, 1htr in next st, 1dc in each of next 5 sts, 1htr in next st, 1dc in each of next 8 sts, join with a ss in first htr. Fasten off.

Right ear:
Work as given for Left ear until 2nd round has been completed.

3rd round: 1dc in each of first 8 sts, 1htr in next st, 1dc in each of next 5 sts, 1htr in next st, 2tr in next st, 1tr in next st, 2tr in next st, 1tr in each of next 2 sts, 1htr in next st, join with a ss in first dc. Fasten off.

Trunk:
With 4.00mm (UK 8) hook and B, make a magic circle (see Note on page 66) and make 1ch, then work 4dc in ring. 4 sts.
Work with WS facing (RS outside).
1st–4th rounds: 1dc in each st to end.
5th round: (2dc in next st, 1dc in next st) twice. 6 sts.
6th round: (2dc in next st, 1dc in each of next 2 sts) twice, join with a ss in first dc. 8 sts. Fasten off.

BEAR CHARM:
Head:
With 4.00mm (UK 8) hook and C, work as given for Elephant charm head.
Ears: (make 2)
With 4.00mm (UK 8) hook and C, make 4ch and work 7tr in 4th ch from hook. Fasten off.
Bow:
With 4.00mm (UK 8) hook and D, make a magic circle

(see Note on page 66) as given for Elephant charm head. (Make 3ch, then work 2tr, 3ch and 1ss in ring) twice, work 7ch. Fasten off. Pull end of yarn gently to close ring. Wrap 7ch twice around centre of bow, thread tail into yarn needle and neatly secure in place.

TIGER CHARM:
Head:
With 4.00mm (UK 8) hook and F, work as given for Elephant charm head.
Ears: (make 2)
With 4.00mm (UK 8) hook and F, make 4ch.
1st row: 1dc in 2nd ch from hook, 1dc in each of next 2ch, turn.
2nd row: Miss first dc, 1dc in each of next 2dc, turn.
3rd row: Miss first dc, 1dc in next dc. Fasten off.
Thread tail into a yarn needle and take tail along edge of triangle so that it exits at position of first ch. Tie two tails in a knot and cut short tail, leaving long tail for sewing ear to head.

MONKEY CHARM:
Head:
With 4.00mm (UK 8) hook and G, work as given for Elephant charm head.
Ears: (make 2)
With 4.00mm (UK 8) hook and G, work as given for Elephant charm head until 2nd round has been completed.
3rd round: Ss in each st to end. Fasten off.

Making up

ELEPHANT CHARM:
Position and pin ears on sides of head and sew in place. Sew trunk in position in centre of face. Take excess yarn B through top of head and cut close to head so that a tuft of 'hair' is left. Loosen a few fibres to give a fuzzy effect. Using a strand of yarn E, sew bead eyes in place. Sew on tiny pink felt patches for cheeks with running stitch. Sew charm lanyard in place on top of head.

BEAR CHARM:
Position and pin ears on sides of head and sew in place. Using photograph as a guide, use neat running stitches and matching thread to sew on a circle of baby pink felt to centre of face for a muzzle and two tiny pink felt patches for cheeks. Using a strand of yarn E, embroider nose in straight stitches on to muzzle, then sew on beads for eyes. Sew bow firmly to head in front of one ear. Sew charm lanyard in place on top of head.

TIGER CHARM:
Position and pin ears on sides of head and sew in place. Using photograph as a guide, position and pin tiny ovals of white felt where eyes will be. Using a strand of yarn E, sew beads for eyes through ovals to anchor them to head. With 4 strands of E, embroider nose in straight stitches in centre of face, with an inverted V shape for mouth. Position small baby pink felt circles for cheeks under eyes and stitch whiskers over cheeks with 4 strands of E to hold them in place. Embroider forehead marking with long straight stitches, one vertically towards nose and 3 horizontally. Sew charm lanyard in place on top of head.

MONKEY CHARM:
Sew a cream felt circle to centre of each ear with running stitch. Position and pin ears on sides of head and sew in place. Using photograph as a guide, cut face shape from cream felt and add face details as foll: using a strand of yarn E, sew on beads for eyes and then embroider nose in straight stitches and a curved, smiling mouth in backstitch. Sew face shape in position on head with running stitches. Sew on small pink felt circles at either side of face for cheeks. Sew charm lanyard in place on top of head.

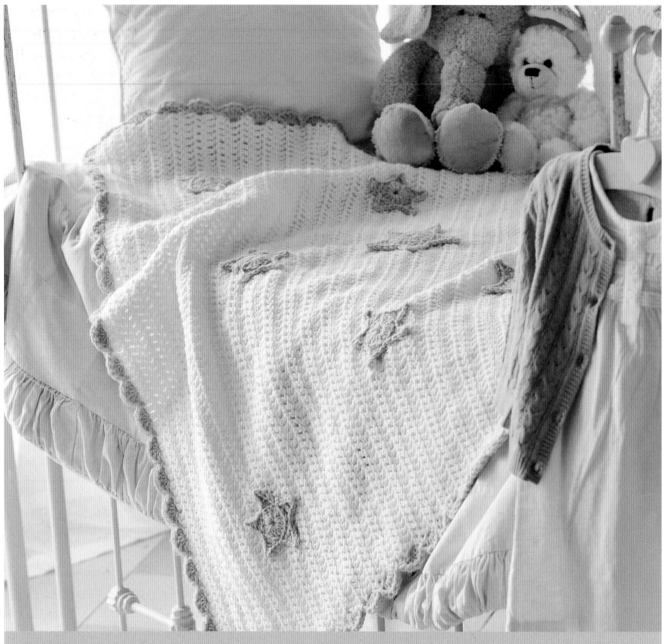

Child's star throw

This lovely throw is very easy to make and you can add however many stars you like.

Soft, cosy and ideal for a child's room, this pastel-coloured throw has a shell edging in a contrast colour and star motifs appliquéd onto the background.

The Yarn

Sirdar Supersoft Aran (approx. 236m/257 yards per 100g/3½oz ball) contains 100% acrylic. It produces an attractive fabric, ideal for projects intended for babies and children as it can be machine washed and tumble-dried. There is a good colour selection.

GETTING STARTED

★ *Background is basic treble fabric, while stars decorations are easy to make.*

Size:
Approximately 94 x 122cm (37 x 48in)

How much yarn:
5 x 100g (3½oz) balls of Sirdar Supersoft Aran in colour A – Cream (shade 831)
2 balls of colour B – Duck Egg Blue (shade 826)

Hooks:
4.00mm (UK 8) crochet hook, 6.00mm (UK 4) crochet hook

Tension:
11 sts and 7.5 rows measure 10cm (4in) square over tr on 6.00mm (UK 4) hook
IT IS ESSENTIAL TO WORK TO THE STATED TENSION TO ACHIEVE SUCCESS

What you have to do:
Work throw in main colour in rows of trebles. Add shell edging in contrast colour. Make large and small stars in rounds using contrast colour. Sew on stars.

Instructions

Abbreviations:

ch = chain(s)
cm = centimetre(s)
cont = continue
dc = double crochet
dtr = double treble
foll = follow(s)(ing)
htr = half treble
patt = pattern
rem = remaining
rep = repeat
RS = right side
ss = slip stitch
st(s) = stitch(es)
tr = treble
tr tr = triple treble
WS = wrong side

THROW:

With 6.00mm (UK 4) hook and A, make 103ch.

Foundation row: (RS) 1tr into 4th ch from hook, 1tr into each ch to end, turn. 101 sts.

Patt row: 3ch (counts as first tr), miss st at base of ch, 1tr into each st to end, working last tr into 3rd of 3ch, turn. Rep last row 88 times, ending with a WS row. Fasten off.

Edging:

With 6.00mm (UK 4) hook and RS of work facing, join B to last st worked and cont as foll: 1ch, ss into first st, *miss next st, 5tr into foll st, miss next st, ss into foll st *, rep from * to * across sts of top, **5tr into next row-end, ss into foll row-end,

5tr into next row-end, miss foll row-end, ss into next row-end **, rep from ** to ** to lower edge, cont across rem 2 sides as before, join with a ss into first ch. Fasten off.

SMALL STAR:
(make 11)
With 4.00mm (UK 8) hook and B, make 4ch, join with a ss into first ch to form a ring.
1st round: 3ch (counts as first tr), work 14tr into ring, join with a ss into 3rd of 3ch.
2nd round: *Loosely work 5ch, working into straight strand that runs across back of each ch work: 1dc into 2nd ch from hook, 1htr into next ch, 1tr into foll ch, 1dtr into next ch, miss next 2tr on ring, ss into foll tr, rep from * 4 more times, working last ss into base of first 5ch. Fasten off.

LARGE STAR: (make 5)
With 4.00mm (UK 8) hook and B, make 5ch, join with a ss into first ch to form a ring.
1st round: 4ch (counts as first dtr), work 19dtr into ring, join with a ss into 4th of 4ch.
2nd round: *Loosely work 6ch, working into straight strand that runs across back of each ch work: 1dc into 2nd ch from hook, 1htr into next ch, 1tr into foll ch, 1dtr into next ch, 1tr-tr into foll ch, miss next 3dtr on ring, ss into foll dtr, rep from * 4 more times, working last ss into base of first 6ch. Fasten off.

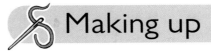

Making up

Position stars on throw as required and using A, sew in place around WS of outer edge, taking care that sts do not show on RS of stars.

Rag doll

Here is a crochet version of a traditional rag doll – she's
soft, cuddly and definitely fun to have around.

GETTING STARTED

★★ *Easy stitches but care is needed with construction for a professional result.*

Size:
Doll measures 50cm (19¾in) tall

How much yarn:
1 x 50g (1¾oz) ball of Sirdar Calico DK in each of five colours: A – Muslin (shade 724); B – Lobster (shade 715); C – Lime Canvas (shade 727); D – Spicy (shade 716) and E – Banana (shade 733)

Hook:
3.50mm (UK 9) crochet hook

Additional items:
Washable polyester toy filling
2 small rubber bands
70cm (¾ yard) of 9mm- (⅜ in-) wide red ribbon
2 blue or black buttons for eyes
Oddment of red stranded embroidery thread

Tension:
18 sts and 22 rows measure 10cm (4in) square over dc on 3.50mm (UK 9) hook
IT IS ESSENTIAL TO WORK TO THE STATED TENSION TO ACHIEVE SUCCESS

What you have to do:
Work body, legs, arms and head in rounds of double crochet, adding stripes to legs and arms and adding stuffing as described. Cut and thread lengths of yarn through head to make plaits and fringe. Work facial details as described. Make dress in double crochet.

The Yarn
Sirdar Calico DK (approx. 158m/172 yards per 50g/1¾oz ball) is a blend of 60% cotton and 40% acrylic. It can be machine washed. The colour pallette includes both pastel and bright shades.

Our charming doll has long limbs, cute features, flaxen hair with plaits and a pretty dress. Worked in a soft, cotton-rich yarn, she can be washed if necessary.

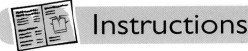 Instructions

Abbreviations:
beg = beginning **ch** = chain **cm** = centimetre(s)
cont = continue **dc** = double crochet
dc2tog = work 2dc together as foll: (insert hook in next st, yrh and draw a loop through) twice, yrh and draw through all 3 loops on hook **dec** = decreasing
foll = follows **inc** = increasing **rep** = repeat
RS = right side **sp** = space **ss** = slip stitch
st(s) = stitch(es) **tog** = together
WS = wrong side **yrh** = yarn round hook

Note: When working stripes on arms and legs, it is impossible to darn in ends. Therefore work a few sts over ends at beg of round and then carefully snip off.

BODY:
With 3.50mm (UK 9) hook and A, make 6ch, join with a ss in first ch to form a ring.
1st round: 1ch (does not count as a st), 6dc in ring, join with a ss in first dc.
Cont in rounds, working first dc of each round in same dc as ss at end of previous round.
2nd round: 1ch, 2dc in each dc to end, join with a ss into

Cont in rounds of dc, work 24 rounds in total, working in stripe patt of 4 rounds B and 2 rounds C. Change to A and work a further 6 rounds.

Shape foot:

Next round: 1ch, (1dc in each of next 3dc, 2dc in next dc) 3 times, join with a ss in first dc. 15 sts.

Next round: 1ch, (1dc in each of next 4dc, 2dc in next dc) 3 times, join with a ss in first dc. 18 sts.

Next round: 1ch, (1dc in each of next 5dc, 2dc in next dc) 3 times, join with a ss in first dc, changing to D on last st. 21 sts.

Shoe:

Next round: With D, 1ch, (1dc in each of next 6dc, 2dc in next dc) 3 times, join with a ss in first dc. 24 sts.
Work 4 rounds in dc.

Next round: 1ch, (1dc in each of next 4dc, dc2tog) 4 times, join with a ss in first dc. 20 sts.

Next round: 1ch, (1dc in each of next 3dc, dc2tog) 4 times, join with a ss in first dc. 16 sts.

Next round: 1ch, (dc2tog) 8 times, join with a ss in first dc. 8 sts.

Next round: 1ch, (dc2tog) 4 times, join with a ss in first dc. 4 sts. Fasten off leaving a long end. Use end to sew last 4 sts tog and secure end of shoe. Stuff this leg and upper half of body.

Second leg:

Rejoin B to inside edge of first leg.

Next round: 1ch, 1dc into each of next 12dc, join with a ss into first dc.

Complete to match first leg, adding more filling to remainder of body and second leg as work progresses.

ARMS: (make 2)

With 3.50mm (UK 9) hook and A, make 2ch.

1st round: 6dc in 2nd ch from hook, join with a ss in first dc.

Cont in rounds, working first dc of each round in same dc as ss at end of previous round.

2nd and 3rd rounds: As 2nd and 3rd rounds of Body. 18 sts.

4th and 5th rounds: Work in dc.

6th–11th rounds: 1ch, 1dc in next dc, dc2tog, 1dc in each dc to end, join with a ss in first dc. 12 sts.

12th and 13th rounds: Work in dc, changing to C on last st. Work 17 more rounds in stripes of 1 round C and 3 rounds B. Fasten off.

Lightly fill arms and then oversew open ends tog to contain filling. Sew arms securely to sides of body.

first dc. 12 sts.

3rd round: 1ch, (1dc in next dc, 2dc in next dc) 6 times, join with a ss in first dc. 18 sts.

4th round: 1ch, (1dc in each of next 2dc, 2dc in next dc) 6 times, join with a ss in first dc. 24 sts.

5th round: 1ch, (1dc in each of next 3dc, 2dc in next dc) 6 times, join with a ss into first dc. 30 sts.

6th round: 1ch, (1dc in each of next 9dc, 2dc in next dc) 3 times, join with a ss in first dc. 33 sts.

7th round: 1ch, (1dc in each of next 10dc, 2dc in next dc) 3 times, join with a ss in first dc. 36 sts.

8th–13th rounds: Cont as set, inc 3 sts on each round. 54 sts.*

**14th round: 1ch, (1dc in each of next 7dc, dc2tog) 6 times, join with a ss in first dc. 48 sts.

15th round: 1ch, (1dc in each of next 6dc, dc2tog) 6 times, join with a ss in first dc. 42 sts

16th–18th rounds: Cont as set, dec 6 sts on each round. 24 sts.**

19th–24th rounds: 1ch, 1dc in each dc to end, join with a ss in first dc, changing to B on last st.

First leg:

Next round: With B, 1ch, 1dc in each of next 6dc, miss next 12dc, 1dc in each of last 6dc, join with a ss in first dc. 12 sts.

HEAD:

Work as given for Body to *.

Work 2 rounds in dc, then work as given for Body from ** to **.

Next round: 1ch, (1dc in each of next 2dc, dc2tog) 6 times, join with a ss in first dc. 18 sts.

Next round: 1ch, (1dc in next dc, dc2tog) 6 times, join with a ss in first dc. 12 sts.

Stuff head firmly.

Next round: 1ch, (dc2tog) 6 times, join with a ss in first dc. Fasten off leaving a long end.

Use end to sew head securely to top of body, working through sts 3 rounds up from last round on head and first round on body.

Hair:

For plaits, cut 60cm lengths of E. Beg at centre top of head, fold each length of E in half and, using crochet hook, pull a length through at regular intervals either side of centre, as if making a fringe. Now make another row in same way, just inside this first line and then along lower back edge of head and at sides of forehead.

Make lengths into two long plaits and secure with rubber bands, approximately 6cm from ends. (If head is not adequately covered by hair, undo plaits and add a few more lengths of E as required.) Trim ends neatly.

Cut red ribbon into two and tie neat bows at ends of plaits to cover rubber bands.

For fringe, cut 20cm (8in) lengths of E. Using 2 at a time, fold in half and pull through first round on top of head. Trim fringe level.

Face:

Using photograph as a guide, sew on buttons (or for babies and toddlers, use small circles of felt instead of buttons) for eyes. Using red embroidery thread, add a curved mouth securing at intervals with small sts and then work 2 small French knots for nose.

DRESS:

Back and front: (alike)

With 3.50mm (UK 9) hook and E, make 50ch.

**1st row: (RS) 1dc in 2nd ch from hook, *miss 3ch, 9tr into next ch, miss 3ch, 1dc in next ch, rep from * to end, do not turn.

2nd row: With RS facing, work back along foundation ch as foll: 1ch (does not count as a st), 1dc in last dc, 3dc in each 3ch sp to end, 1dc in first dc at beg of previous row. ** 38 sts. Change to D.

3rd row: With D, 1ch, 1dc in each dc to end, turn.

Work 19 more rows in dc.

Shape bodice:

Next row: (WS) 1ch, 1dc in first dc, (dc2tog) 18 times, 1dc in last dc, turn. 20 sts.

Work 6 rows in dc.

Shape armholes:

Next row: (RS) Ss in each of first 4dc, 1ch, 1dc in each of next 12dc, turn. 12 sts.

Work 5 rows in dc.

Shape neck:

Next row: (RS) 1ch, 1dc in each of first 5dc, turn and complete this side of neck first.

Next row: 1ch, miss first dc, 1dc in each of next 4dc, turn.

Next row: 1ch, 1dc in each of first 3dc. Fasten off.

With RS facing, miss 2dc at centre front neck, join yarn in next st, 1ch, 1dc in same dc as join, 1dc in each of next 4dc, turn.

Next row: 1ch, 1dc in each of first 4dc, turn.

Next row: 1ch, miss first dc, 1dc in each of next 3dc. Fasten off. Join one shoulder seam.

With 3.50mm (UK 9) hook, E and RS facing, work 21dc evenly around neck edge. Fasten off.

SLEEVES: (make 2)

With 3.50mm (UK 9) hook and E, make 26ch. Work as given for Back and front from ** to **. 20 sts.

Change to D.

Next row: With D, 1ch, (1dc in each of next 3dc, 2dc in next dc) 4 times, 1dc in each of next 4dc, turn. 24 sts.

Work 7 rows in dc.

Next row: 1ch, 1dc in each of first 2dc, (dc2tog) 10 times, 1dc in each of last 2dc. Fasten off.

POCKET:

With 3.50mm (UK 9) hook and D, make 5ch.

1st row: 2dc in 2nd ch from hook, 2dc in each ch to end. 8 sts.

Work 7 rows in dc. Change to E and work 1 more row. Fasten off.

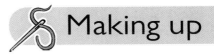 Making up

Sew pocket on to front of dress as shown. Sew one sleeve into armhole, then join underarm and side seam. Place half-finished dress on to doll and join shoulder seam. Now sew remaining sleeve into armhole, then join remaining underarm and side seam.

Child's hooded jacket

Give your tiny tot an early start in the style stakes with this cute striped jacket.

Worked in double crochet with chic stripes, this hooded jacket has a boxy shape with stylish drawstring fastenings for the hood, cuff and lower edges. It can be made for a boy or a girl.

The Yarn

Sublime Organic Cotton DK (approx. 110m/120 yards per 50g/1¾oz ball) contains 100% organic cotton. It is a natural, untreated yarn that can be machine washed. There is a range of soft and matt colours to choose from.

GETTING STARTED

★★ Basic fabric is easy to work but needs a lot of attention to details of design.

Size:

To fit chest: 51[56:61]cm (20[22:24]in)
Actual size: 62[66.5:71]cm (24½[26¼:28]in)
Length to shoulder: 33[38:43]cm (13[15:17]in)
Sleeve seam: 25[28:31]cm (10[11:12¼]in)
Note: Figures in square brackets [ ] refer to larger sizes; where there is only one set of figures, it applies to all sizes

How much yarn:

4[4:5] x 50g (1¾oz) balls of Sublime Organic Cotton DK in colour A – Rice Pudding (shade 98)
3[4:4] balls in colour B – Drift (shade 140)
3[3:4] balls in colour C – Pea Pod (shade 91)

Hooks:

3.50mm (UK 9) crochet hook,
4.00mm (UK 8) crochet hook

Additional items:

4[5:5] x 15mm (⅝in) buttons,
20cm (8in) of 6mm- (¼in-) wide elastic
Sewing needle and thread

Tension:

18 sts and 20 rows measure 10cm (4in) square over dc on 4.00mm (UK 8) hook
IT IS ESSENTIAL TO WORK TO THE STATED TENSION TO ACHIEVE SUCCESS

What you have to do:

Work throughout in double crochet and stripe pattern. Make inserted front pockets with linings and shaped edges as instructed. Make casings for drawstrings around hood, cuff and lower edges. Make twisted cords for drawstrings.

Instructions

Abbreviations:

beg = beginning **ch** = chain(s)
cm = centimetre(s)
cont = continue **st(s)** = stitch(es);
dc = double crochet
dc2tog = into each of next 2 sts work: (insert hook into st, yrh and draw through a loop), yrh and draw through all 3 loops on hook
foll = follows **inc** = increase
patt = pattern **RS** right side
rem = remaining **rep** = repeat;
sp = space **ss** = slip stitch
tog = together **WS** = wrong side
yrh = yarn round hook

BACK:

With 4.00mm (UK 8) hook and A, make 57[61:65]ch.
Foundation row: (RS) 1dc in 2nd ch from hook, 1dc in each ch to end, turn. 56[60:64] sts.
1st row: 1ch (counts as first st), miss st at base of ch, 1dc into each dc to end, working last dc in turning ch, turn.
Rep last row throughout.
Cont in stripe sequence of 6 more rows A (8 rows A in total), 2 rows C, 8 rows B and 2 rows C until 64[74:84] rows in all have been completed, ending with 4 rows A[B:A].

Shape shoulders:

Cont in same colour.
1st row: Ss into each of first 4[4:5] sts, 1ch, patt to last 3[3:4] sts, turn.
2nd row: Ss into each of first 4[5:5] sts, 1ch, patt to last 3[4:4] sts, turn.
3rd row: Ss into each of first 5 sts, 1ch, patt to last 4 sts, turn.
4th row: As 3rd row. 28[30:32] sts. Fasten off.

POCKET LINING: (make 2)

With 4.00mm (UK 8) hook and A, make 23[24:25]ch. Work foundation row as given for Back. 22[23:24] sts. Now work

9 more rows in stripes to match Back, ending with 2 rows C. Fasten off.

LEFT FRONT:

With 4.00mm (UK 8) hook and A, make 27[29:31]ch. Work foundation row as given for Back. 26[28:30] sts. Now work 9 more rows in stripes to match Back, ending with 2 rows C. Fasten off. **

Pocket front:

With RS facing, join B to 5th[6th:7th] st, 1ch, 1dc in each dc to end, working last dc in turning ch, turn. 22[23:24] sts.

Next row: (WS) 1ch, miss first dc, 1dc in each dc to last 2dc, dc2tog, turn, leaving 1ch unworked.

Next row: 1ch, miss dc2tog, 1dc in each dc, working last dc in turning ch, turn. 20[21:22] sts. Keeping stripes correct, rep last 2 rows 7 times more, then work first of them again, ending with 8 rows A. 4[5:6] sts. Fasten off.

With RS of both pieces facing, place one pocket lining behind pocket front, matching lower and left side edges (hold in place with a safety-pin). Join B to last st of 10th row of Front.

Side joining row: 1ch, miss first dc, 1dc into each of 3[4:5] dc left unworked, then work 22[23:24]dc across top edge of pocket lining. 26[28:30]dc.

Work 17 rows more in stripes, ending with 8 rows A.

Top joining row: Changing to C, work to last 4[5:6] sts, then hold top edge of pocket front in front of rem sts and work last 4[5:6]dc through both edges tog. Cont in stripes until 58[68:78] rows in all have been completed, ending with 8 rows B[A:B].

Shape neck and shoulder:

Cont in stripes, beg 2 rows C.

1st row: 1ch, miss first dc, 1dc in each of next 19[20:21] dc, dc2tog over next 2dc, turn leaving 4[5:6] sts unworked. 21[22:23] sts.

2nd row: 1ch, miss dc2tog, 1dc in each dc, working last dc in turning ch, turn.

3rd row: 1ch, miss first dc, 1dc in each dc to last 2dc, dc2tog, turn leaving turning ch unworked. 19[20:21] sts. Rep last 2 rows once more, then work 2nd row again. 17[18:19] sts.

7th row: Ss into each of first 4[4:5] sts, 1ch, 1dc in each dc to last 2dc, dc2tog, turn.

8th row: 1ch, miss dc2tog, 1dc in each dc to last 3[4:4] sts, turn.

9th row: Ss into each of first 5 sts, 1ch, 1dc in each dc, leaving turning ch unworked. Fasten off.

RIGHT FRONT:

Work as given for Left front to **.

Pocket front:

Change to B as set.

Next row: Patt to last 6[7:8] sts, dc2tog, turn. 21[22:23] sts.

Next row: (WS) 1ch, miss dc2tog, 1dc in each dc, working last dc in turning ch, turn.

Next row: 1ch, miss first dc, 1dc in each dc to last 2dc, dc2tog, turn leaving turning ch unworked. 19[20:21] sts. Keeping stripes correct, rep last 2 rows 7 times more, then work first of them again, ending with 8 rows A. Fasten off.

With RS of both pieces facing, place one pocket lining behind pocket front, matching lower and right side edges. Join B to last st of 10th row of pocket lining.

Side joining row: 1ch, miss first dc, 1dc in each dc across top edge of pocket lining, 1dc in each of 4[5:6] sts left unworked on 11th row of Right front. 26[28:30]dc.

Work 17 rows more in stripes, ending with 8 rows in A.

Top joining row: Changing to C, hold top edge of pocket front tog with first 5[6:7] sts, 1ch, miss 1dc on each edge, work 4[5:6]dc through both edges tog, then work 21[22:23]dc to end of row, turn. 26[28:30] sts. Cont in stripes until 58[68:78] rows in all have been completed, ending with 8 rows B[A:B].

Shape neck and shoulder:

1st row: Join C to 5th[6th:7th] st, 1ch, 1dc in each dc, working last dc in turning ch, turn. 22[23:24] sts.

2nd row: 1ch, miss first dc, 1dc in each dc to last 2dc, dc2tog, turn leaving turning ch unworked. 20[21:22] sts.

3rd row: 1ch, miss dc2tog, 1dc in each dc, working last dc in turning ch, turn. Rep last 2 rows once more, then work 2nd row again. 16[17:18] sts.

7th row: 1ch, miss dc2tog, 1dc in each dc to last 3[3:4] sts, turn.

8th row: Ss into each of first 4[5:5] sts, 1ch, 1dc in each dc to last 2dc, dc2tog, turn leaving turning ch unworked.

9th row: 1ch, 1dc in each of 3dc. Fasten off.

SLEEVES: (make 2)

With 4.00mm (UK 8) hook and A, make 33[35:37]ch. Work foundation row as given for Back. 32[34:36] sts.

Now work 3 rows in dc.

Inc row: 1ch, 1dc in first dc, 1dc in each dc to turning ch, 2dc in turning ch, turn. 1 st inc at each end of row. Beg 3 more rows in A, cont in stripes and inc 1 st at each end of every foll 4th row until there are 50[54:58] sts. Work straight in stripes until 48[54:60] rows have been completed in all, ending 8 rows A[4 rows B:2 rows C]. Fasten off.

HOOD:

Join shoulder seams.

With 4.00mm (UK 8) hook and C, make 34[38:42]ch. Fasten off and leave aside.

With 4.00mm (UK 8) hook and RS facing, join C at right front neck edge, 1ch, work 14[15:16]dc along neck edge to shoulder seam, then work in prepared ch as foll: 1dc in each of 34[38:42] ch, then work 15[16:17]dc along left front neck from shoulder seam to front edge. 64[70:76] sts. Work 1 row in dc. Cont in stripes, beg 8 rows B, for a further 30 rows, ending with 2 rows C.

Shape top of hood:
First side: Join in A.
1st row: 1ch, miss first dc, 1dc in each of next 21dc, dc2tog, turn. Work on these 23 sts only.
2nd row: 1ch, miss dc2tog, 1dc in each dc, working last dc in turning ch, turn.
3rd row: 1ch, miss first dc, 1dc in each dc to last 2dc, dc2tog, turn leaving 1ch unworked. 21 sts. Rep last 2 rows twice more, then work 2nd row again. Fasten off.
Centre section: With RS of hood facing, rejoin A to same place as last st of 1st row of first side, 1ch, 1dc in each of next 16[22:28]dc, turn. 17[23:29] sts. Cont in stripes, beg 7 more rows A, for a further 27 rows, ending with 8 rows A. Fasten off.
Second side: With RS of hood facing, rejoin yarn to same place as last st of 1st row of centre section, 1ch, 1dc in each dc, working last dc in turning ch, turn. 25 sts.
2nd row: 1ch, miss first dc, 1dc in each dc to last 2dc, dc2tog, turn leaving turning ch unworked. 23 sts.
3rd row: 1ch, miss dc2tog, 1dc in each dc, work last dc in turning ch, turn. Rep last 2 rows twice more, then work 2nd row again. Fasten off.

 Making up

Mark position for sleeves 14[15:16.5]cm down from each shoulder seam. Sew in sleeves between markers. Join side and sleeve seams. Join seams at top of hood, easing in first and second sides to fit centre section. Join hood to back neck.
Buttonhole band (for a boy):
With 3.50mm (UK 9) hook and RS of left front facing, join C to neck corner.
1st row: 1ch, 1dc in side edge of each row to corner. 58[68:78] sts.
2nd row: 1ch, miss first dc, 1dc in each st, working last dc in turning ch, turn.
3rd row: 1ch, miss first dc, 1dc in each of next 2dc, *2ch, miss 2dc, 1dc in each of next 13dc, rep from * 2[3:3] times more, 2ch, miss 2dc, 1dc in each of next 7[2:12]dc, 1dc in turning ch, turn.
4th row: 1ch, miss first dc, *1dc in each dc to 2ch sp, dc2tog inserting hook in same place as last dc, then in 2ch sp, dc2tog inserting hook in 2ch sp, then in next dc, 1dc in same place as hook last inserted, rep from * to last 2 sts, 1dc in next dc, 1dc in turning ch, turn.
5th and 6th rows: As 2nd row. Fasten off.
Buttonhole band (for a girl):
Work as given for boy's version but on right front edge and working buttonholes as foll:
3rd row: 1ch, miss first dc, 1dc in each of next 7[2:12]dc, *2ch, miss next 2dc, 1dc in each of next 13dc, rep from * 2[3:3] times more, 1dc in each of next 2dc, 1dc in turning ch, turn.

4th row: Work as given for boy's version to last 7[2:12] sts, 1dc into each dc, 1dc into turning ch, turn.
Button band (both versions):
Work as given for buttonhole band on opposite front edge, omitting buttonholes.
Pocket borders: (make 2)
With 3.50mm (UK 9) hook and RS facing, join C to right end of pocket slit.
1st row: 1ch, 1dc in side edge of each row to end of slit, turn. Work 1 more row in dc. Fasten off.
Cuffs: (make 2)
With 3.50mm (UK 9) hook and RS facing, join to base of sleeve seam.
1st row: 1ch, 1dc in base of each st all round, turn. Work 2 rows in dc.
4th row: 1ch, 1dc in back loop only of each dc, working last dc in turning ch, turn. Work 2 more rows in dc. Fasten off leaving a long end. Fold cuff to RS of sleeve and use yarn end to slipstitch each st of last row to corresponding st of 1st row.
Lower border:
With 3.50mm (UK 9) hook and RS facing, join C halfway across lower edge of left front band.
1st row: 1ch, 1dc in side edge of each row of band and 1dc in base of each st all around, ending at centre of lower edge of right front band. Complete to match cuffs. Neatly slipstitch pocket linings in place on inside of jacket. Catch down ends of pocket borders.
Hood border:
With 3.50mm (UK 9) hook and RS facing, join C to right front of hood at neck edge.
1st row: 1ch, 1dc in side edge of each row and in each dc across centre top, around to left front neck edge, turn. Complete to match cuffs.
Drawstrings:
For waist drawstring, make a twisted cord from a 6m (6½-yard) length of C. Double length, tie two ends tog and pin to a firm surface, or loop around a door handle. Twist opposite end between your fingers until strands are very tightly wound all along, then put your finger at centre of cord and bring two ends tog. Allow cord to spiral. Tie a knot at end with previous knot and run cord through fingers to even out spiral. Use a safety-pin to thread smooth end of cord through lower border, then knot smooth end of cord and trim both ends into a tassel.
For hood, make a drawstring from a 5.2m (17-foot) length of C. For cuffs, make four drawstrings from 1.5m (5m) lengths. For each cuff, cut 10cm (4in) of elastic and sew smooth end of drawstring to each end of elastic.
Thread through cuff and tie in a bow. (Cuffs need not be untied once correct fit is obtained.)

Embellished bunting

Hang out the flags with this pretty pastel bunting.

Worked in four pastel shades of cotton yarn and embellished with toning trimmings and embroidery, this pretty bunting is easy to make – and you can keep adding extra pennants to create the length that you require.

The Yarn
Debbie Bliss Cotton DK (approx. 84m/92 yards per 50g/1¾oz ball) contains 100% pure cotton. It produces a soft fabric with good stitch definition that can be machine washed. There is a wide palette of pastels and strong colours.

GETTING STARTED

 Pennants are easy to work in double crochet.

Size:
Each pennant measures 12cm (4¾in) wide x 15cm (6in) high; finished length of string, approx 2.7m (9ft)

How much yarn:
1 x 50g (1¾oz) ball of Debbie Bliss Cotton DK in each of four colours: A – Duck Egg (shade 09); B – Pink (shade 16); C – Green (shade 20) and D – Cream (shade 02)

Hook:
4.00mm (UK 8) crochet hook

Additional items:
*Selection of complementary-coloured trims, such as small buttons, ribbon and lace
Sewing needle and thread*

Tension:
*15 sts and 18 rows measure 10cm (4in) square over dc on 4.00mm (UK 8) hook
IT IS ESSENTIAL TO WORK TO THE STATED TENSION TO ACHIEVE SUCCESS*

What you have to do:
Work each pennant in double crochet, starting at point and increasing as directed. Work some pennants in two-row stripes of all four colours. Crochet circular flower motifs for some pennants. Make double crochet string and border connecting pennants along their top edge. Sew on series of decorative touches with trimmings.

Instructions

Abbreviations:

ch = chain(s)

cm = centimetre(s)

cont = continue

dc = double crochet

rep = repeat

sp(s) = space(s)

ss = slip stitch

st(s) = stitch(es)

tr = treble

WS = wrong side

Note: To make a Magic Circle, wrap yarn clockwise around forefinger twice to form a ring. Holding end of yarn between thumb and middle finger, insert hook into ring and draw yarn from ball through.

PENNANT:

With 4.00mm (UK 8) hook make 2ch.

Foundation row: (WS) 1dc in 2nd ch from hook, turn.

Next row: 1ch (does not count as a st), 2dc in st at base of ch, turn. 2 sts.

Next row: 1ch, 1dc in each dc, turn.

Next row: 1ch, 2dc in each st, turn. 4 sts.

Cont in dc, work 2 rows straight.

Next row: 1ch, 2dc in first st, 1dc in each st to last st, 2dc in last st, turn. 6 sts.

Work 2 rows straight.

Rep last 3 rows until there are 18 sts and 26 rows in all have been completed. Fasten off.

Make a total of 12 pennants – 3 in each of A, B and C, plus 3 more in stripe sequence of 2 rows each A, B, C and D, fastening off at end of each stripe.

FLOWER MOTIF:

(make 3)

With B, make a magic circle (see Note left).

Foundation round: With 4.00mm (UK 8) hook, work 6dc into ring, join with a ss into first dc and pull yarn to tighten ring.

1st round: *2ch, ss into next dc, rep from * 4 times more, 2ch, join with a ss into first dc of Foundation round.

6 ch sps. Fasten off.

2nd round: Join in D to first ch sp, into each ch sp work (1ss, 1ch, 3tr, 1ch, 1ss), join with a ss into first ss. Fasten off.

Sew a flower to each striped pennant.

TIES AND BAND:

With 4.00mm (UK 8) hook and D, make 45ch, join with a ss to top left-hand corner of a pennant in B and fasten off.

Join D to top right-hand corner of same pennant in B,

make 9ch and join with a ss to top left-hand corner of a pennant in A and fasten off.

Join D to top right-hand corner of same pennant in A, make 9ch and join with a ss to top left-hand corner of a pennant in C and fasten off.

Join D to top right-hand corner of same pennant in C, make 9ch and join with a ss to top left-hand corner of a striped pennant and fasten off.

Cont in this way in colour sequence as set until all pennants have been joined.

Join D to top right-hand corner of last striped pennant and make 46ch, 1dc into 2nd ch from hook, 1dc into each ch and each dc along top of pennants to end. Fasten off.

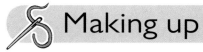

Making up

Using sewing thread, sew ribbon and lace in a cross formation to each pennant in B. Sew a selection of buttons and ribbon bows to each pennant in A. Using A and B, work lazy daisy flowers with buttons at their centre to each pennant in C.

Toy tractor

Destined to be a firm favourite in the toy box, this chunky tractor is up for hours of fun.

Tractor-lovers, young and old, will adore this crochet version. Worked in double crochet throughout, its details are embroidered on afterwards.

The Yarn

Patons Diploma Gold DK (approx. 120m/136 yards per 50g/1¾oz ball) is a blend of 55% wool, 25% acrylic and 20% nylon. It combines the good looks of wool with the practical qualities of man-made fibres, which makes it ideal for toy projects. There is a wide shade range.

GETTING STARTED

★★ *Easy basic fabric but involves colour work techniques and precise making up for a professional finish.*

Size:
Finished size (without wheels):
22cm (8½in) long x 21cm (8¼in) tall x 8cm (3¼in) wide

How much yarn:
1 x 50g (1¾oz) ball of Patons Diploma Gold DK in each of four colours: A – Thyme (shade 06213); B – Apple Green (shade 06125); C – Honey (shade 06228) and D – White (shade 06187)
2 balls in colour E – Black (shade 06183)

Hook:
4.00mm (UK 8) crochet hook

Additional items:
Washable polyester wadding
22 x 21cm (8½ x 8¼in) block of upholstery foam, 8cm (3¼in) thick

Tension:
18 sts and 19 rows measure 10cm (4in) square over dc on 4.00mm (UK 8) hook
IT IS ESSENTIAL TO WORK TO THE STATED TENSION TO ACHIEVE SUCCESS

What you have to do:
Work throughout in double crochet. Work side and centre panels in rows, with stripes and coloured blocks as directed. Use intarsia techniques for colour work. Work wheels in rounds.

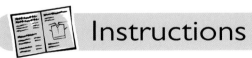 Instructions

Abbreviations:

ch = chain(s); **cm** = centimetre(s); **cont** = continue **dc** = double crochet; **dc2tog** = into each of next 2 sts, work as foll: (insert hook into st, yrh and draw a loop through), yrh and draw through all 3 loops on hook; **foll** = follows; **rep** = repeat; **RS** = right side **ss** = slip stitch; **st(s)** = stitch(es); **WS** = wrong side **yrh** = yarn round hook

Note: Before starting work, wind off a small ball of A to use when working cab.

RIGHT SIDE PANEL:

With 4.00mm (UK 8) hook and A, make 40ch.

Foundation row: (RS) 1dc into 2nd ch from hook, 1dc into each ch to end, turn.

1st row: 1ch (does not count as a st), 1dc into each st to end, turn. 39 sts.

Rep last row 11 times more.*

Next row: (WS) 1ch, 1dc into each of next 19 sts, change to C, 1dc into each of next 20 sts, turn.

Next row: With C, 1ch, 1dc into each of next 20 sts, change to A, 1dc into each of next 19 sts, turn.

Next row: 1ch, 1dc into each of next 19 sts, change to B, 1dc into each of next 20 sts, turn.

Next row: With B, 1ch, 1dc into each of next 20 sts, change to A, 1dc into each of next 19 sts, turn.

Next row: 1ch, 1dc into each of next 19 sts, change to B, 1dc into each st to last 2 sts, dc2tog, turn.

Next row: With B, 1ch, miss first st, 1dc into each of next 18 sts, change to A, 1dc into each st to end, turn. Fasten off B.

Shape cab:

Next row: (WS) With A, 1ch, 1dc into each of next 19 sts, turn.

Use a separate ball of A for each side of window. Always join in new colour on last part of previous st.

Next row: With A, 1ch, 1dc into each of next 4 sts, with D, 1dc into each of next 12 sts, with small ball of A, 1dc into each of next 3 sts, turn.

Next row: With A, 1ch, 1dc into each of next 3 sts, with D, 1dc into each of next 12 sts, with A, 1dc into each of next 4 sts, turn.

Rep last 2 rows 7 times more, then with A only, work 1 row across all sts.

Next row: 1ch, miss first st, 1dc into each st to last 2 sts, dc2tog, turn.

Rep last row twice more. Fasten off.

LEFT SIDE PANEL:

Work as given for Right side to *. Fasten off A.

Next row: (WS) With C, 1ch, 1dc into each of next 20 sts, change to A, 1dc into each of next 19 sts, turn.

Next row: With A, 1ch, 1dc into each of next 19 sts, change to C, 1dc into each of next 20 sts, turn.

Next row: With B, 1ch, 1dc into each of next 20 sts, change to A, 1dc into each of next 19 sts, turn.

Next row: With A, 1ch, 1dc into each of next 19 sts, change to B, 1dc into each of next 20 sts, turn.

Next row: With B, 1ch, miss first st, 1dc into each of next 19 sts, change to A, 1dc into each of next 19 sts, turn.

Next row: With A, 1ch, 1dc into each of next 19 sts, change to B, 1dc into each st to last 2 sts, dc2tog. Fasten off B.

Shape cab:

With WS facing, return to A and draw a loop through adjacent st in B on right.

Next row: 1ch, 1dc into each of next 19 sts, turn.

Next row: With A, 1ch, 1dc into each of next 3 sts, with D, 1dc into each of next 12 sts, with small ball of A, 1dc into each of next 4 sts, turn.

Next row: With A, 1ch, 1dc into each of next 4 sts, with D, 1dc into each of next 12 sts, with A, 1dc into each of next 3 sts, turn.

Rep last 2 rows 7 times more, then with A only, work 1 row across all sts, turn.

Next row: 1ch, miss first st, 1dc into each st to last 2 sts, dc2tog, turn.

Rep last row twice more. Fasten off.

CENTRE PANEL:

With 4.00mm (UK 8) hook and A, make 13ch.

Foundation row: (RS) 1dc into 2nd ch from hook,

1dc into each ch to end, turn.

1st row: 1ch (does not count as a st), 1dc into each st to end, turn. 12 sts.

Rep last row 31 times more.

Cont in dc as before, work in stripes as foll: 2 rows C, 27 rows B, 14 rows D, 20 rows B, 14 rows D, 20 rows B and 20 rows A. Fasten off.

BACK WHEELS: (make 2)
Front:

With 4.00mm (UK 8) hook and C, make 2ch.

1st round: 6dc into 2nd ch from hook, join with a ss into first dc.

2nd round: 1ch (does not count as a st), (2dc into next st) 6 times, join with a ss into first dc. 12 sts.

3rd round: 1ch, (1dc into next st, 2dc into next st) 6 times, join with a ss into first dc. 18 sts.

4th round: 1ch, (1dc into each of next 2 sts, 2dc into next st) 6 times, join with a ss into first dc. 24 sts.

5th round: 1ch, (1dc into each of next 3 sts, 2dc into next st) 6 times, join with a ss into first dc. 30 sts.

Change to E.

6th round: 1ch, (1dc into each of next 4 sts, 2dc into next st) 6 times, join with a ss into first dc. 36 sts.

7th round: 1ch, (1dc into each of next 5 sts, 2dc into next st) 6 times, join with a ss into first dc. 42 sts.

8th round: 1ch, (1dc into each of next 6 sts, 2dc into next st) 6 times, join with a ss into first dc. 48 sts.

9th round: 1ch, (1dc into each of next 7 sts, 2dc into next st) 6 times, join with a ss into first dc. 54 sts.

10th round: 1ch, (1dc into each of next 8 sts, 2dc into next st) 6 times, join with a ss into first dc. 60 sts.*

11th round: 1ch, 1dc into each st to end, join with a ss into first dc, turn.

12th round: 2ch, 1htr into each st to end, join with a ss into first htr, turn.

Rep last round 4 times more. Fasten off.

Back:

Using E only throughout, work as given for Front to *. Fasten off.

FRONT WHEELS: (make 2)
Front:

With 4.00mm (UK 8) hook and C, make 2ch.

1st round: 6dc into 2nd ch from hook, join with a ss into first dc.

2nd round: 1ch (does not count as a st), (2dc into next st) 6 times, join with a ss into first dc. 12 sts.

Change to E.

3rd–6th rounds: As given for 3rd–6th rounds of Back wheels. 36 sts.**

7th round: 1ch, 1dc into each st to end, join with a ss into first dc, turn.

Rep last round 4 times more. Fasten off.

Back:

Using E only throughout, work as given for Front to **. Fasten off.

HEADLAMPS: (make 2)

With 4.00mm (UK 8) hook and D, make 2ch.

1st round: 6dc into 2nd ch from hook, join with a ss into first dc.

2nd round: 1ch, 2dc into each st to end, join with a ss into first dc. 12 sts.

3rd round: 1ch, 1dc into each st to end, join with a ss into first dc.

Rep last round twice more. Fasten off, leaving a long end. Thread cut end through last round and pull up tight. Sew headlamps to centre panel, just below stripe in C.

✂ Making up

With E, outline windows on right and left side panels in backstitch, continuing down front edge of window to starting ch edge. With two strands of E, work a horizontal straight stitch for door handle on each panel. Work three long vertical stitches on each panel for exhaust grill, placing them two rows down and one stitch in from stripe in C. Work backstitch along top and bottom edges of windows in centre panel.

Place one side panel onto piece of upholstery foam and cut to shape. Join first and last rows of centre panel to form a ring. Placing this seam at centre of lower edge and matching stripe in C and windows, sew centre panel to side panels, leaving one lower edge open. Insert foam, slipstitch opening closed.

Cut three pieces of wadding to same size as each wheel. Place wadding inside front of each wheel and then sew back of wheel in place. Sew wheels firmly in place to tractor using picture as a guide to positioning them.

Baby Henley sweater

Bright colours are used for this mini version of a grown-up favourite.

With contrast-coloured borders and trims, this miniature version of an adult classic sweater makes a stylish addition to baby's wardrobe.

GETTING STARTED

★★ *Easy stitch pattern but take care with details for a good result.*

Size:

To fit chest: *46[51:56:61]cm (18[20:22:24]in)*

Actual size: *50[54:62:67]cm (19¾[21¼:24½:26½]in)*

Length: *26[28:30:32]cm (10¼[11:11¾:12½]in)*

Sleeve seam: *16[18:20:22]cm (6¼[7:8:8½]in)*

Note: *Figures in square brackets [ ] refer to larger sizes; where there is only one set of figures, it applies to all sizes*

How much yarn:

2[3:3:4] x 50g (1¾oz) balls of Sirdar Calico DK in colour A – Spicy (shade 716)

1 ball in colour B – Banana (shade 733)

Hook:

4.00mm (UK 8) crochet hook

Additional item:

4 buttons

Tension:

18.5 sts and 22 rows measure 10cm (4in) square over patt on 4.00mm (UK 8) hook

IT IS ESSENTIAL TO WORK TO THE STATED TENSION TO ACHIEVE SUCCESS

What you have to do:

Work lower edges, cuffs, borders and mock pocket top in double crochet in contrast colour. Work main fabric and collar in half treble and slip stitch pattern. Divide for front opening and shape neck and sleeves as directed.

The Yarn

Sirdar Calico DK (approx. 158m/172 yards per 50g/1¾oz ball) is 60% cotton and 40% acrylic. It makes a soft fabric with good stitch definition. Machine-washable and available in a wide colour range.

 Instructions

BACK:

With 4.00mm (UK 8) hook and B, make 47[51:59:63]ch.

Foundation row: (RS) 1dc in 2nd ch from hook, 1dc in each ch to end, turn. 46[50:58:62]dc.

Next row: 1ch (does not count as a st), 1dc in each dc to end, turn.

Rep last row twice more. Cut off B.

Join in A and cont in patt as foll:

1st row: (RS) 2ch (counts as first htr), miss st at base of ch, ss in next dc, *1htr in next dc, ss in next dc, rep from * to end, turn.

2nd row: 2ch, miss st at base of ch, ss in next htr, *1htr in next ss, ss in next htr, rep from * to end, working last ss in 2nd of 2ch, turn.

Rep last row throughout to form patt until work measures 26[28:30:32]cm (5½[11:11¾:12½]in) from beg, ending with a WS row. Fasten off.

FRONT:

Work as given for Back until Front measures 14[16:18:20]cm (5½[6¼:7:8]in) from beg, ending with a WS row.

Divide for front opening:

Next row: 2ch, miss st at base of ch, ss in next

Abbreviations:

beg = beginning
ch = chain(s)
cm = centimetre(s)
cont = continue
dc = double crochet
dc2tog = (insert hook in next st, yrh and draw a loop through) twice, yrh and draw through all 3 loops on hook
dec = decreased
foll = follows
htr = half treble
inc = increase(d)
patt = pattern
rem = remain(ing)
rep = repeat
RS = right side
ss = slip stitch
st(s) = stitch(es)
WS = wrong side
yrh = yarn round hook

htr, (1htr in next ss, ss in next htr) 9[10:12:13] times, turn.
Cont on these 20[22:26:28] sts for first side of opening for a further 7cm (2¾in), ending with a WS row.

Shape neck:

1st row: 2ch, miss st at base of ch, ss in next htr, (1htr in next ss, ss in next htr) 8[9:11:12] times, turn. 18[20:24:26] sts

2nd row: Ss in each of first 3 sts, 2ch,

miss st at base of ch, ss in next htr, patt to end, turn. 16[18:22:24] sts.

3rd row: 2ch, miss st at base of ch, ss in next htr, (1htr in next ss, ss in next htr) 6[7:9:10] times, turn. 14[16:20:22] sts.

4th row: As 2nd. 12[14:18:20] sts.
Work straight in patt until Front matches Back to shoulder, ending with a WS row. Fasten off.

With RS of work facing, return to base of opening, miss 6 sts at centre front, rejoin yarn to next st, 2ch, miss st at base of ch, ss in next htr, patt to end, turn. Cont on these 20[22:26:28] sts until second side of neck opening matches first, ending with a WS row.

Shape neck:

1st row: Ss in each of first 3 sts, 2ch, miss st at base of ch, ss in next htr, patt to end, turn. 18[20:24:26] sts.

2nd row: 2ch, miss st at base of ch, ss in next htr, (1htr in next ss, ss in next htr) 7[8:10:11] times, turn. 16[18:22:24] sts.

3rd row: As 1st. 14[16:20:22] sts.

4th row: 2ch, miss st at base of ch, ss in next htr, (1htr in next ss, ss in next htr) 5[6:8:9] times, turn. 12[14:18:20] sts.
Work straight in patt until Front matches Back to shoulder, ending with a WS row. Fasten off.

SLEEVES: (make 2)

With 4.00mm (UK 8) hook and B, make 25[25:31:31] ch. Work foundation row as given for Back (24[24:30:30] sts), then work 2 rows in dc.

Next row: 1ch, 1dc in first dc, (2dc in next dc, 1dc in each of next 2dc) 7[7:9:9] times, 2dc in next dc, 1dc in last dc, turn. 32[32:40:40] dc. Cut off B.

Join in A and work 4 rows in patt as given for Back.

Inc row: 3ch, ss in 3rd ch from hook, 1htr in next st (last ss on previous row), ss in next htr, *1htr in next ss, ss in next htr, rep from * to end, working last ss in 2nd of 2ch, turn. 2 sts inc at beg of row.

Rep last row once more. 36[36:44:44] sts. Work 3[3:4:5] rows straight, then work inc row twice. Rep last 5[5:6:7] rows 3 times more. 52[52:60:60] sts. Work straight until Sleeve measures 16[18:20:22]cm from beg, ending with a WS row. Fasten off.

FRONT BORDERS:

With 4.00mm (UK 8) hook and RS facing, join A to top of left side of front opening, 1ch, then work 15dc evenly down left side of opening, 6dc across base of opening and 15dc up right side of opening. Fasten off.

Button band:

With 4.00mm (UK 8) hook and RS facing, join B to top of left side of opening, 1ch, 1dc in each of 15dc down side of opening, turn. Work 3 more rows in dc. Fasten off.

Buttonhole band:

With 4.00mm (UK 8) hook and RS facing, join B to bottom of right side of opening, 1ch, 1dc in each of 15dc up right side of opening, turn. Work 1 more row in dc.

Buttonhole row: 1ch, 1dc in each of first 2dc, (1ch, miss next dc, 1dc in each of next 4dc) twice, 1ch, miss next dc, 1dc in each of last 2dc, turn.

Work 1 more row in dc, working 1dc in each 1ch space. Fasten off.

COLLAR:

Join shoulder seams.

With 4.00mm (UK 8) hook and RS of work facing, join B to top corner of right front border, 1ch, work 4dc along row-ends of border, 17dc up right front neck, 22dc across back neck, 17dc down left front neck and 4dc along row-ends of left front border, turn. 64dc.

Next row: Ss in each of first 3dc, 2ch, miss st at base of ch, ss in next dc, *1htr in next dc, ss in next dc, rep from * to last 2 sts, turn. 60 sts.

Cont in patt as given for Back, work a further 11 rows.

Next row: 1ch, 1dc in each st to end. Fasten off.

MOCK POCKET TOP:

With 4.00mm (UK 8) hook and B, make 14ch.

Work foundation row as given for Back (13 sts), then work 1 row in dc.

Next row: 1ch, miss st at base of ch, 1dc in each dc to last 2dc, dc2tog, turn. 1 st dec at each end of row.

Rep last row until 3 sts rem.

Next row: 1ch, miss st at base of ch, dc2tog. Fasten off.

Edging:

With 4.00mm (UK 8) hook and RS facing, rejoin B to beg of foundation row, 1ch, then work in dc evenly along two sloped edges. Fasten off.

SIDE BORDERS:

Insert markers on side edges of Back and Front, 14 rows up from top of lower edging.

With 4.00mm (UK 8) hook, B and RS facing, work 15dc evenly between marker and bottom of lower edging. Work 1 more row in dc. Fasten off.

Remove markers.

Making up

Insert markers 14[14:16:16]cm (5½[5½:6¼:6¼]in) down from shoulder seams on back and front. Sew in top of sleeves between markers. Join side seams, from top of borders, and sleeve seams. Overlapping side borders on front over those on back, catch top edges in place. Overlapping buttonhole band over button band, sew row ends in place to bottom of front opening.

With RS facing, place foundation ch edge of mock pocket top on left side of front, level with 2nd buttonhole with point facing upwards towards shoulder. Sew straight edge in place. Fold pocket over to cover seam and secure to front by sewing on a button. Sew on rem 3 buttons to button band.

Baby papoose

Buttoned in safely, any baby will love
the cosy security of this soft lined pouch.

Worked in the softest yarn and stripes of beautiful colours that coordinate with the fabric lining, this gorgeous accessory for a baby has button flaps for easy access and is trimmed with a picot edging and pretty braid.

GETTING STARTED

★★ *Pattern is rows of basic stitches and stripes but care is needed with making up lining for a professional finish.*

Size:
Approximately 35cm (14in) wide x 70cm (27½in) long, when fastened

How much yarn:
2 x 50g (1¾oz) balls of Sublime Baby Cashmere Merino Silk DK in each of five colours: A – Gooseberry (shade 04); B – Vanilla (shade 03); C – Jammy (shade 102); D – Smitten (shade 49) and E – Cuddle (shade 02)

Hook:
4.00mm (UK 8) crochet hook

Additional items:
1m (1 yard) of printed cotton lining fabric (we used Cath Kidston "Electric Flowers")
4 m (4½ yards) of braid or ribbon
11 buttons
Sewing thread and needle

Tension:
11 sts measure 7cm (2¾in) and 10 rows measure 7.5cm (3in) over htr on 4.00mm (UK 8) hook
IT IS ESSENTIAL TO WORK TO THE STATED TENSION TO ACHIEVE SUCCESS

What you have to do:
Work throughout in random stripes of double crochet and half trebles as directed. When working stripes, always change to new colour on last part of stitch in old colour. Cut lining fabric to shape of crochet piece as directed. Sew on braid to cover raw edges of lining fabric.

The Yarn
Sublime Baby Cashmere Merino Silk DK (approx. 116m/126 yards per 50g/1¾oz ball) is a blend of 75% merino wool, 20% silk and 5% cashmere. It is soft and smooth on a baby's skin and can be machine washed. There is a good colour range to team with printed fabric.

Instructions

Abbreviations:
ch = chain(s)
cm = centimetre(s)
cont = continue
dc = double crochet
foll = follows
htr = half treble
rep = repeat
RS = right side
sp = space
ss = slip stitch
st(s) = stitch(es)
WS = wrong side

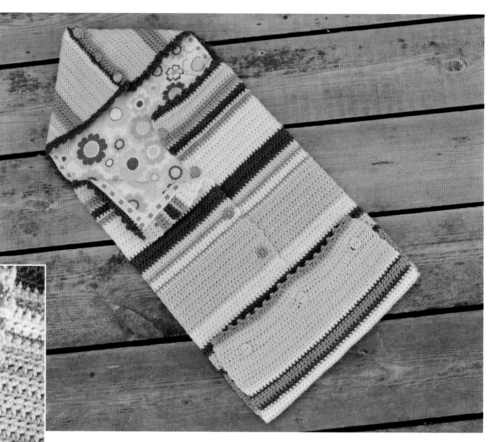

POUCH:
Lower flap:
With 4.00mm (UK 8) hook and A, make 53ch loosely.

Foundation row: (RS) 1htr into 3rd ch from hook, 1htr into each ch to end, turn. 52 sts.

Next row: 2ch (counts as first htr), miss st at base of ch, 1htr into each st to end, working last htr into 2nd of 2ch, turn.

Work 1 more row in htr.

1st buttonhole row: 2ch, miss st at base of ch, 1htr into each of next 6 sts, (1ch, miss next st, 1htr into each of next 18 sts) twice, 1ch, miss next st, 1htr into each st to end, turn.

2nd buttonhole row: Work in htr, working 1htr into each 1ch sp.

Work 5 more rows in htr changing to B on last part of last st in A.

Next row: With B, 1ch (counts as first dc), miss st at base of ch, 1dc into each st to end, working last dc into top of turning ch, turn.

Work 1 more row in dc, changing to C on last part of last st in B.

Always changing to new colour on last part of last st in old colour, cont as foll:

With C, work 1 row in dc.
With D, work 2 rows in htr.
With C, work 1 row in dc.
With B, work 3 rows in dc.
With E, work 1 row in htr.

Shape for front flaps:
Next 2 rows: With E, make 31ch, 1htr into 3rd ch from hook, 1htr into each of next 28ch, 1htr into each st to end, turn. 112 sts.

*1st buttonhole row: (RS) With E, 2ch, miss st at base of ch, 1htr into each of next 2 sts, 1ch, miss next st, 1htr into each st to end, changing to D on last part of last st, turn.

2nd buttonhole row: With D, work in htr, working 1htr into 1ch sp.*

With D, work 9 more rows in htr.

With C, work 1 row in dc.

1st buttonhole row: With C, 1ch, miss st at base of ch, 1dc into each of next 2 sts, 2ch, miss next 2dc, 1dc into each st to end, changing to A on last part of last st, turn.

2nd buttonhole row: With A, work in dc, working 2dc into 2ch sp and changing to E on last part of last st, turn.

With E, work 2 rows in htr.

With A, work 1 row in dc.

With C, work 3 rows in dc.

With B, work 4 rows in htr.

With E, work 2 rows in htr.

With E, make buttonhole as given from * to *, working both rows in E.

With E, work 6 more rows in htr.

With A, work 2 rows in dc.

With D, work 1 row in dc.

With B, work 2 rows in htr, changing to D on last part of last st.

1st buttonhole row: (WS) With D, work in dc to last 5 sts, 2ch, miss next 2 sts, 1dc into each of next 2 sts, 1dc into top of turning ch, changing to A on last part of st, turn.

2nd buttonhole row: With A, work in dc, working 2dc into 2ch sp.

With A, work 2 more rows in dc.

With C, work 4 rows in htr.

With B, work 5 rows in htr.

With B, make buttonhole as given from * to *, working both rows in B.

With B, work 3 more rows in htr.

With D, work 2 rows in dc.

With E, work 1 row in dc.

With C, work 2 rows in htr.

With E, work 1 row in dc.

With D, work 3 rows in dc.

With A, make buttonhole as given from * to *, working both rows in A.

With A, work 2 more rows in htr. Fasten off.

Hood:

With RS facing, join C to 31st st from buttonhole edge, 2ch, miss st at base of ch, 1htr into each of next 51 sts, turn.

Work 9 rows in htr on these 52 sts.

With E, work 2 rows in dc.

With B, work 1 row in dc.

With A, work 2 rows in htr.

With B, work 1 row in dc.

With E, work 3 rows in dc.

With D, work 4 rows in htr.

With A, work 10 rows in htr.

With B, work 1 row in dc.

Shape for buttonhole flap:

Next row: With B, 1ch, miss st at base of ch, 1dc into each of next 24 sts, turn.

With C, work 1 row in dc on these 25 sts.

1st buttonhole row: With D, 1ch, miss st at base of ch, 1dc into each of next 2dc, (2ch, miss next 2 sts, 1dc into each of next 7 sts) twice, 2ch, miss next 2 sts, work in dc to end, turn.

2nd buttonhole row: Work in dc, working 2dc into each 2ch sp. Work 1 more row in dc. Fasten off.

Edging:

With 4.00mm (UK 8) hook and WS of work facing, join D to other side of foundation ch at lower flap and work 1ch, 1dc into each st on other side of foundation ch, turn. 52 sts.

Picot row: 1ch (does not count as a st), *1dc into each of next 2 sts, 3ch, ss into last dc made, miss next dc, rep from * to last st, 1dc into last st.

Fasten off.

With C, work a similar picot edging (with multiples of 3 sts + 1) along top edges of front flaps and up side edges of hood (will form face edge of hood when fastened).

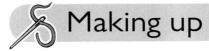 Making up

Sew in all loose ends.

Lay crochet pouch out flat with WS uppermost. Lay WS of lining fabric on top and carefully cut lining around shape of crochet piece, approximately 1cm (½in) inside all edges and buttonhole lines. Pin lining in place. Lay strips of braid along all edges of lining, hiding raw edges of fabric. Using sewing thread and needle, slipstitch inner edges of braid in place through lining fabric and catching loops of crochet. Then slipstitch outer edges of braid in place to secure to crochet. Sew on buttons to correspond with buttonholes, noting that central button for flap is also used for front fastening.

Alphabet letters

These big tactile ABC letters make a great three-part present for the baby in your life.

Worked in double crochet and half trebles in five attractive shades of baby yarn, these three-dimensional letters are great fun whether displayed on a shelf or used for play.

GETTING STARTED

 Easy to make, but constructing letters and adding filling requires patience.

Size:
Finished height of each letter is approximately 16cm (6¼in)

How much yarn:
1 x 50g (1¾oz) ball of Sirdar Snuggly Baby Bamboo DK in each of five colours: A – Limey (shade 155); B – Sailboat (shade 156); C – Yellow Submarine (shade 157); D – Jellybaby (shade 153) and E – Cream (shade 131)

Hook:
3.50mm (UK 9) crochet hook

Additional item:
Washable polyester toy filling

Tension:
20 sts and 20 rows measure 10cm (4in) square over dc on 3.50mm (UK 9) hook
IT IS ESSENTIAL TO WORK TO THE STATED TENSION TO ACHIEVE SUCCESS

What you have to do:
Work mainly in double crochet, shaping as directed. For each letter, make two sides in different colours, plus outer and inner gussets. Sew pieces together with blanket stitch in a contrasting colour. Use toy filling to give letters a three-dimensional effect.

The Yarn
Sirdar Snuggly Baby Bamboo DK (approx. 95m/104 yards per 50g/1¾oz ball) is a blend of 80% bamboo-sourced viscose and 20% wool. It is machine-washable and comes in a range of shades.

Instructions

LETTER A:
First side:
With 3.50mm (UK 9) hook and A, make 72ch.
1st row: 1dc into 2nd ch from hook, 1dc into each of next 32ch, dc2tog, 1dc into next dc, dc2tog, 1dc into each of next 33ch, turn. 69 sts.
2nd row: 1ch (does not count as a st), dc2tog, 1dc into each of next 30dc, dc2tog, 1dc into next dc, dc2tog, 1dc into each of next 30dc, dc2tog, turn. 65 sts.
3rd row: 1ch, 1dc into each of next 30dc, dc2tog, 1dc into next dc, dc2tog, 1dc into each of next 30dc, turn. 63 sts.
4th row: 1ch, dc2tog, 1dc into each of next 27dc, dc2tog, 1dc into next dc, dc2tog, 1dc into each of next 27dc, dc2tog, turn. 59 sts.
5th row: 1ch, 1dc into each of next 27dc, dc2tog, 1dc into next dc, dc2tog, 1dc into each of next 27dc, turn. 57 sts.
6th row: 1ch, dc2tog, 1dc into each of next 23dc, dc3tog, 1dc into next dc, dc3tog, 1dc into each of next 23dc, dc2tog, turn. 51 sts.
7th row: 1ch, 1dc into each of next 22dc, dc3tog, 1dc into next dc, dc3tog, 1dc into each of next 22dc, turn. 47 sts.
Second side:
With B, work as given for First side.
Cross bar:
With 3.50mm (UK 9) hook and A, make 12ch for lower edge.
1st row: 1dc into 2nd ch from hook, 1dc into each ch to end, turn.
2nd row: 1ch (does not count as a st), dc2tog, 1dc into each dc to last 2 sts, dc2tog, turn.
3rd row: 1ch (does not count as a st), 1dc into each dc, turn.
4th row: As 2nd row. Fasten off.
With B, work second Cross bar to match.
Leaving 4.5cm (1¾in) at each end of last row of first side free, sew matching Cross bar to First side.

Abbreviations:

ch = chain(s)
cm = centimetre(s)
dc = double crochet
dc2(3)tog = (insert hook into next st, yrh and draw a loop through) 2(3) times, yrh and draw through all 3(4) loops on hook
htr = half treble
rep = repeat
ss = slip stitch
st(s) = stitch(es)
tr = treble
yrh = yarn round hook

Outer gusset:

With 3.50mm (UK 9) hook and C, make 6ch.

1st row: 1dc into 2nd ch from hook, 1dc into each ch to end, turn. 5 sts.

2nd row: 1ch (does not count as a st), 1dc into each dc to end, turn.

Rep last row until band fits around both outer sloping edges of letter.

Change to D and cont until this section fits around underneath letter and back to first corner. Fasten off.

Inner gusset:

With E, work as given for Outer gusset until strip fits around inner triangle above Cross bar. Fasten off.

LETTER B:
First side:

With 3.50mm (UK 9) hook and C, make 31ch.

1st row: 1dc into 2nd ch from hook, 1dc into each ch to end, turn. 30 sts.

2nd row: 1ch (does not count as a st), 1dc into each dc to end, turn.

Rep last row 3 times more.

Shape curves:

1st row: Ss into each of first 5dc, 18ch, miss next 9dc, 1tr into each of next 2dc, 18ch, miss next 9dc, ss into next dc, turn.

2nd row: 1ch, 1dc into each of next 18ch, 1dc into each of next 2tr, 1dc into each of next 18ch, turn.

3rd row: 1ch, 1dc into each of next 5 sts, 1htr into next st, (2htr into next st, 1htr into next st) 3 times, 1dc into each of next 5 sts, (dc2tog) twice, 1dc into each of next 5 sts, 1htr into next st, (2htr into next st, 1htr into next st) 3 times, 1dc into each of last 5 sts, turn.

4th row: 1ch, 1dc into each of next 6 sts, 1htr into next st, (2htr into next st, 1htr into next st) 4 times, 1dc into each of next 4 sts, (dc2tog) twice, 1dc into each of next 4 sts, 1htr into next st, (2htr into next st, 1htr into next st) 4 times, 1dc into each of last 6 sts, turn.

5th row: 1ch, 1dc into each of next 22 sts, (dc2tog) twice, 1dc into each of last 22 sts. Fasten off.

Second side:

With E, work as given for First side.

Outer gusset:

With 3.50mm (UK 9) hook and B, make 6ch.

1st row: 1dc into 2nd ch from hook, 1dc into each ch to end, turn. 5 sts.

2nd row: 1ch (does not count as a st), 1dc into each dc to end, turn.

Rep last row until gusset fits up straight side of letter. Change to D and cont until this section fits around two curves and back round to side edge. Fasten off.

Inner gussets: (make 2)

With A, work 27 rows as given for Outer gusset.

LETTER C:
First side:

With 3.50mm (UK 9) hook and B, make 28ch.

1st row: 1dc into 2nd ch from hook, 1dc into each ch to end, turn. 27 sts.

2nd row: 1ch (does not count as a st), (1dc into next dc, 2dc into next dc) 4 times, 1dc into each of next 11dc, (2dc into next dc, 1dc into next dc) 4 times, turn. 35 sts.

3rd row: 1ch, 1dc into next dc, 2dc into next dc, (1dc into each of next 2dc, 2dc into next dc) 3 times, 1dc into each of next 13dc, (2dc into next dc, 1dc into each of next 2dc) 3 times, 2dc into next dc, 1dc into last dc, turn. 43 sts.

4th row: 1ch, 1dc into next dc, 2dc into next dc, (1dc into each of next 3dc, 2dc into next dc) 3 times, 1dc into each of next 15dc, (2dc into next dc, 1dc into each of next 3dc) 3 times, 2dc into next dc, 1dc into last dc, turn. 51 sts.

5th row: 1ch, 1dc into next dc, 2dc into next dc, (1dc into each of next 4dc, 2dc into next dc) 3 times, 1dc into each of next 17dc, (2dc into next dc, 1dc into each of next 4dc) 3 times, 2dc into next dc, 1dc into last dc, turn. 59 sts.

6th row: 1ch, 1dc into next dc, 2dc into next dc, (1dc into each of next 5dc, 2dc into next dc) 3 times, 1dc into each of next 19dc, (2dc into next dc, 1dc into each of next 5dc) 3 times, 2dc into next dc, 1dc into last dc, turn. 67 sts.

7th row: 1ch, 1dc into each dc to end. Fasten off.

Second side:

With D, work as given for First side.

Gusset:

With 3.50mm (UK 9) hook and A, make 6ch.

1st row: 1dc into 2nd ch from hook, 1dc into each ch to end, turn. 5 sts.

2nd row: 1ch, 1dc into each dc to end, turn. Rep last row until band fits around outer curve of letter.

Change to C and cont until this section fits around inner curve and back round to starting point. Fasten off.

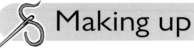 Making up

LETTER A:

Join row ends of inner gusset to form a ring and place above cross bar. Using a contrast-coloured thread, sew inner gusset in place with blanket stitch. Join short ends of outer gusset and sew in place around outer edges of letter, using blanket stitch. Sew other side of letter to gussets in same way, leaving a gap in seam. Stuff with toy filling and blanket stitch opening closed.

LETTER B:

Sew row ends of curves in place. Join row ends of inner gussets to form two rings and using a contrast-coloured yarn, sew to insides of curves on one side of letter with blanket stitch. Join short ends of outer gusset to form a ring and, using contrast-coloured yarn, sew in place around outer edges of letter, using blanket stitch. Sew other side in place in same way, leaving a small opening in one side. Stuff with the toy filling and then blanket stitch opening closed.

LETTER C:

Join ends of gusset to form a ring. Using a contrast-coloured yarn, sew gusset in place to one side of letter with blanket stitch. Sew other side in place in the same way, leaving a small opening in one outer seam. Stuff with toy filling and then blanket stitch opening closed.

Toy elephant

Children will love playing with this delightful Indian elephant, complete with blanket and headdress.

Cute in cotton yarn and double crochet in two shades of grey and cheerful green, this elephant toy with a colourful patterned blanket is bound to be a winner.

The Yarn

Anchor Style Creativa and Magicline (both approx. 70m/ 76 yards per 50g/1¾oz ball) contain 100% cotton. Creativa is a mercerised cotton with a slight lustre and great colour range, while working with variageted Magicline produces instant patterns.

GETTING STARTED

★★ *Easy stitches but construction needs care and patience.*

Size:
Height to shoulder: approximately 18cm (7in)
How much yarn:
2 x 50g (1¾oz) balls of Anchor Style Creativa in colour A – pale grey (shade 00398)
1 ball in colour B – Dark Grey (shade 00235)
1 x 50g (1¾oz) ball of Anchor Style Magicline in colour C – green dotty (shade 01496)
Hook:
3.50mm (UK 9) crochet hook
Additional items:
Washable polyester toy filling
2 small domed buttons for eyes
5cm (2in) square of thin ivory felt
Ivory sewing thread and sewing needle
Tension:
16 sts and 20 rows measure 10cm (4in) square over dc on 3.50mm (UK 9) hook
IT IS ESSENTIAL TO WORK TO THE STATED TENSION TO ACHIEVE SUCCESS
What you have to do:
Work elephant in double crochet throughout, either in rows or rounds, and shaping as described. Insert toy filling at various stages of construction as directed. Make blanket and head-piece in chevron pattern.

 # Instructions

HEAD AND BODY:
Trunk:
With 3.50mm (UK 9) hook and A, make 10ch, join with a ss in 1st ch to form a ring.
1st round: (WS) 1ch (does not count as a st), working in back strand of each ch only, 1dc in each ch to end, ss in 1st dc, turn.
2nd round: 1ch, 1dc in 1st dc, (dc2tog) 4 times, 1dc in last dc, ss in 1st dc, turn. 6 sts.
3rd round: 1ch, 1dc in each dc, ss in 1st dc, turn.
Rep last round 4 times more.

8th round: 1ch, 2dc in 1st dc, 1dc in each dc to last dc, 2dc in last dc, ss in 1st dc, turn. 8 sts.
Rep last round twice more. 14 sts.
Next round: (WS) 1ch, 1dc in each dc to end, do not join, turn. Cont in dc, working in rows not rounds, as foll:
Face:
1st row: (RS) 1ch, 2dc in each dc to end, turn. 28 sts.
2nd row: 1ch, 1dc in each st to end, turn.
3rd row: 1ch, 1dc in each of next 9dc, 2dc in each of next 2dc, 1dc in each of next 6dc, 2dc in each of next 2dc, 1dc in each of next 9dc, turn. 32 sts.

Abbreviations:

ch = chain(s)
cm = centimetre(s)
cont = continue
dc = double crochet
dc2tog = (insert hook into next st and draw a loop through) twice, yrh and draw through all 3 loops
foll = follows
rep = repeat
RS = right side
ss = slip stitch
st(s) = stitch(es)
tr = treble
tr2(3)tog = (yrh, insert hook into next st, yrh and draw a loop through, yrh and draw through first two loops) 2(3) times, yrh and draw through all 3(4) loops
WS = wrong side
yrh = yarn round hook

4th row: 1ch, 1dc in each of next 9dc, 2dc in each of next 4dc, 1dc in each of next 6dc, 2dc in each of next 4dc, 1dc in each of next 9dc, turn. 40 sts.

5th and 6th rows: 1ch, 1dc in each dc to end, turn.

Shape cheeks:

Next row: (RS) 1ch, 1dc in first dc, (dc2tog) 3 times, 1dc in each of next 26dc, (dc2tog) 3 times, 1dc in last dc, turn. 34 sts.

Shape mouth:

Next row: Join first 3 and last 3 sts on previous row with ss, 1ch, 1dc in each dc to end, ss in 1st dc to join in a round, turn. 28 sts.

Turning at end of each round, cont as foll:

Next round: 1ch, 1dc in each st to end, ss in 1st dc, turn.

Rep last round 3 times more.

Shape chest and neck:

Next round: (RS) 1ch, 2dc in each of next 3dc, 1dc in each of next 5dc, (dc2tog) twice, 1dc in each of next 4dc, (dc2tog) twice, 1dc in each of next 5dc, 2dc in each of last 3dc, ss in 1st dc, turn. 30 sts.

2nd round: 1ch, 2dc in each of first 3dc, 1dc in each dc to last 3dc, 2dc in each of last 3dc, ss in 1st dc, turn. 36 sts.

3rd round: 1ch, (1dc in each of next 2dc, 2dc in next dc) 3 times, 1dc in each dc to last 9dc, (2dc in next dc, 1dc in each of next 2dc) 3 times, ss in 1st dc, turn. 42 sts. Leaving loop of st ready for working body, now make up and stuff the head as foll: Sew end of trunk together to form a V shape and stuff lightly. Join row ends of face and stitch into a fold just behind trunk. Cut square of ivory felt in half diagonally to make two triangles. Roll each triangle up tightly to form two

cone-shaped tusks and secure with a few sewing sts. Insert points of tusks through sts either side of mouth and pull through as far as possible. Sew securely in place. Insert stuffing around tusks to shape face and stuff. Sew one domed button securely to each side of face, pull thread between them slightly together to form eye sockets. (**Safety note** – if making elephant for a child, instead of buttons, embroider eyes in B.)

Pick up loop left before making up and stuffing head and cont as foll, inserting stuffing as shape narrows:

Body:

Next round: 1ch, 1dc in each dc to end, ss in 1st dc, turn.

Rep last round 10 times more.

Shape tummy:

Next round: (RS) 1ch, 1dc in 1st dc, 2dc in each of next 3dc, 1dc in each dc to last 4dc, 2dc in each of next 3dc, 1dc in last dc, ss in 1st dc, turn. 48 sts.

Next round: 1ch, 1dc in each dc to end, ss in 1st dc, turn.

Rep last round 8 times more.

Shape bottom:

1st round: (RS) 1ch, 1dc in each of next 15dc, (dc2tog, 1dc in each of next 2dc) 5 times, 1dc in each of next 13dc, ss in 1st dc, turn. 43 sts.

2nd round: 1ch, 1dc in each dc to end, ss in 1st dc, turn.

3rd round: 1ch, 1dc in each of next 3dc, (dc2tog, 1dc in each of next 3dc) 8 times, ss in 1st dc, turn. 35 sts.

4th round: 1ch, 1dc in each of next 3dc, (dc2tog, 1dc in each of next 2dc) 8 times, ss in 1st dc, turn. 27 sts.

5th round: 1ch, 1dc in each of next 3dc, (dc2tog, 1dc in each of next 2dc) 6 times, ss in 1st dc, turn. 21 sts.

6th round: 1ch, 1dc in 1st dc, (dc2tog) 10 times, ss in 1st dc. 11 sts.

Finish stuffing body.

7th round: 1ch, 1dc in 1st dc, (dc2tog) 5 times, ss in 1st dc, do not turn. 6 sts.

Tail:

Next round: 1ch, (dc2tog) 3 times, ss in 1st dc2tog. 3 sts.
Cont working in a spiral for 6 more rounds, work 2ch,
fasten off. With B, make a small tassle and sew to end of tail.

LEGS:
Front legs:

With 3.50mm (UK 9) hook and B, make 2ch.
1st round: 6dc in 2nd ch from hook, ss in 1st dc to join.
2nd round: 1ch, 2dc in each dc to end, ss in 1st dc.
3rd round: 1ch, (1dc in next dc, 2dc in next dc) 6 times,
ss in 1st dc. 18 sts.
4th round: 1ch, 1dc in each dc to end, ss in 1st dc, turn.
Rep last round 3 times more.
Shape foot:
Next round: (RS) 1ch, 1dc in each of next 5dc, (dc2tog,
1dc in next dc) 3 times, 1dc in each of last 4dc, ss in 1st
dc, turn. 15 sts.
Next round: 1ch, 1dc in each dc to end, ss in 1st dc,
turn.***
Change to A and rep last round 12 times. Fasten off.
Back legs:
Work a given for Front legs to ***.
Change to A and rep last round 10 times. Fasten off.

EARS:

With 3.50mm (UK 9) hook and B, make 15ch.
1st row: 1dc in 2nd ch from hook, 1dc in each ch to
end, turn. 14 sts.
2nd row: (RS) 1ch, 2dc in each dc to end, turn. 28 sts.
3rd row: 1ch, 1dc in each st to end, turn.
4th row: 1ch, 1dc in each of next 9dc, 2dc in each of
next 2dc, 1dc in each of next 6dc, 2dc in each of next
2dc, 1dc in each of next 9dc, turn. 32 sts.
5th row: 1ch, 1dc in each dc to end. Fasten off.

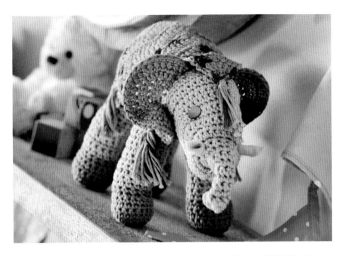

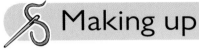
Making up

Stuff legs firmly and sew in place on body. Sew on ears.
Blanket:
With 3.50mm (UK 9) hook and C, make 34ch.
1st row: (RS) 1tr in 4th ch from hook, *1tr in each of
next 3ch, tr3tog over next 3ch, 1tr in each of next 3ch,
3tr in next ch, rep from *, ending last rep with 2tr in last
ch, turn.
2nd row: 3ch (counts as 1tr), 1tr in st at base of ch, *1tr
in each of next 3tr, tr3tog over next 3tr, 1tr in each of
next 3tr, 3tr in next tr, rep from *, ending last rep with
2tr in 3rd of 3ch, turn.
Rep last row 7 times more. Fasten off.
Head decoration:
With 3.50mm (UK 9) hook and C, make 14ch.
1st row: (RS) 1tr in 4th ch from hook, 1tr in each of
next 3ch, tr3tog over next 3ch, 1tr in each of next 3ch,
2tr in last ch, turn.
2nd row: 3ch, miss st at base of ch, 1tr in each of next
3tr, tr3tog over next 3 sts, 1tr in each of next 3tr, 1tr in
3rd of 3ch, turn.
3rd row: 3ch, miss st at base of ch, tr2tog over next 2tr,
tr3tog over next 3 sts, tr2tog over next 2tr, 1tr in 3rd of
3ch, turn.
4th row: 3ch, miss st at base of ch, tr3tog over next 3
sts, 1tr in 3rd of 3ch, turn. Fasten off.
Sew foundation ch edge of head decoration to centre of
last row of blanket.
Make 5 tassles and sew one to point of head decoration
and one to each corner of blanket. Place blanket on
elephant's back and slip stitch in place behind his ears.

Child's baseball jacket

Be right on trend with this classically styled jacket

Classic styling with striped edgings, sleeves in a contrast colour and with an initial motif, this sporty baseball jacket will be popular with boys and girls alike.

GETTING STARTED

This garment has simple stitches and very little shaping, but take care with the details.

Size:

To fit age: 6[8:10] years

Jacket chest measurement: 71.5[81:91]cm (28[32:36]in)

Length: 37[45:53]cm (14½[17¾:21]in)

Sleeve seam: 28[34:40]cm (11[13½:15¾]in)

Note: Figures in square brackets [ ] refer to larger sizes; where there is only one set of figures, it applies to all sizes

How much yarn:

5[5:6] x 50g (1¾oz) balls of Debbie Bliss Rialto DK in colour A – Navy (shade 17)

4[4:5] balls in colour B – White (shade 01)

1 ball in colour C – Red (shade 12)

Hooks:

3.00mm (UK 11) crochet hook

3.50mm (UK 9) crochet hook

4.00mm (UK 8) crochet hook

Additional items:

6 buttons

6 snap fasteners

Sewing thread and needle

Tension:

16.5 sts and 10 rows measure 10cm (4in) square over tr on 4.00mm (UK 8) hook

IT IS ESSENTIAL TO WORK TO THE STATED TENSION TO ACHIEVE SUCCESS

What you have to do:

Work main fabric in trebles throughout. Work edgings in double crochet and stripes as directed. Make letter A separately and sew in place.

The Yarn

Debbie Bliss Rialto DK (approx. 105m/114 yards per 50g/1¾oz ball) is 100% merino wool. It makes a soft, warm fabric, machine-washable at a low temperature. It's likely to have your team colours.

 Instructions

BACK:

With 4.00mm (UK 8) hook and C, make 54[60:68]ch.

Foundation row: (RS) 1dc in 2nd ch from hook, 1dc in each ch to end, turn. 53[59:67] sts.

1st row: 1ch (does not count as a st), 1dc in each dc to end, changing to B on last st, turn.

With B, work 2 rows in dc. Change to C and work 2 more rows in dc. Change to A and cont in A throughout.

Inc row: (RS) 2ch (counts as first tr), miss st at base of ch, (1tr in each of next 5 sts, 2tr in next st) 3[4:4] times, 1tr in each of next 15[9:17] sts, (2tr in next st, 1tr in each of next 5 sts) 3[4:4] times, 1tr in last st, turn. 59[67:75] sts.

Next row: 2ch, miss st at base of ch, 1tr in each st to end, working last tr in 2nd of 2ch, turn.

Work 18[24:30] more rows in tr, ending with a WS row.

Shape armholes:

1st row: (RS) Fasten off yarn, miss first 7 sts, join yarn in next st, 2ch, miss st at base of ch, 1tr in each of next 44[52:60] sts, turn. 45[53:61] sts.

Cont straight in tr for 11[13:15] rows, ending with a WS row.

Shape back neck:

Next row: (RS) 2ch, miss st at base of ch, 1tr in each of next 13[16:19] sts, turn. 14[17:20] sts. Work 1 row in tr. Fasten off.

With RS of work facing, miss centre 17[19:21] sts at base of neck, rejoin yarn in next st, 2ch, miss st at base of ch, 1tr in each st to end, turn. 14[17:20] sts. Work 1 row in tr. Fasten off.

Abbreviations:

beg = begin(ning)
ch = chain(s)
cm = centimetre(s)
cont = continue
dc = double crochet
dc2tog = (insert hook in next st, yrh and draw a loop through) twice, yrh and draw through all 3 loops
foll = following
inc = increase
rem = remaining
RS = right side
ss = slip stitch
st(s) = stitch(es)
tog = together
tr = treble
tr2tog = (yrh, insert hook in next st, yrh and draw a loop through, yrh and draw through first 2 loops) twice, yrh and draw through all 3 loops
WS = wrong side
yrh = yarn round hook

Note:
When changing colour, introduce new colour on last stitch in old colour, working last part of last stitch with new colour.

LEFT FRONT:
With 4.00mm (UK 8) hook and C, make 28[31:35]ch. Work foundation row as given for Back. 27[30:34] sts. Work 5 rows in dc and stripes as given for Back.
Change to A and cont in A throughout.**
Inc row: (RS) 2ch, miss st at base of ch, (1tr in each of next 5 sts, 2tr in next st) 3[4:4] times, 1tr in each of rem 8[5:9] sts, turn. 30[34:38] sts.
Cont straight in tr for 19[25:31] rows, ending with a WS row.
Shape armhole:
1st row: (RS) Fasten off yarn, miss first 7 sts, join yarn in next st, 2ch, miss st at base of ch, 1tr in each st to end, turn. 23[27:31] sts.
Cont straight in tr for 7[7:9] rows, ending with a WS row.
Shape neck:
1st row: (RS) 2ch, miss st at base of ch, 1tr in each of next 14[17:20] sts, tr2tog over next 2 sts, 1tr in next st, turn. 17[20:23] sts.
2nd row: 2ch, miss st at base of ch, tr2tog over next 2 sts, 1tr in each st to end, turn.
3rd row: 2ch, miss st at base of ch, 1tr in each st to last 3 sts, tr2tog over next 2 sts, 1tr in 2nd of 2ch, turn.
4th row: As 2nd. 14[17:20] sts. Cont straight in tr for 2[4:4] rows. Fasten off.

RIGHT FRONT:
Work as given for Left front to **.
Inc row: (RS) 2ch, miss st at base of ch, 1tr in each of next 7[10] sts, (2tr in next st, 1tr in each of next 5 sts) 3[4:4] times, 1tr in last st, turn. 30[34:38] sts.

Cont straight in tr for 19[25:31] rows, ending with a WS row.
Shape armhole:
1st row: (RS) 2ch, miss st at base of ch, 1tr in each of next 22[26:30] sts, turn. 23[27:31] sts.
Cont straight in tr for 7[7:9] rows, ending with a WS row.
Shape neck:
1st row: (RS) Fasten off yarn, miss first 5[6:7] sts, rejoin yarn in next st, 2ch, miss st at base of ch, tr2tog over next 2 sts, 1tr in each st to end, turn. 17[20:23] sts.
Complete to match Left front.

SLEEVES: (make 2)
With 4.00mm (UK 8) hook and C, make 28[30:32]ch. Work foundation row as given for Back. 27[29:31] sts. Work 5 rows in dc and stripes as given for Back, changing to B on last colour change and cont in B throughout.
Inc row: (RS) 2ch, miss st at base of ch, 1tr in each of next 1[2:3] sts, (2tr in next st, 1tr in each of next 2 sts) 3 times, 2tr in next st, 1tr in each of next 3 sts, (2tr in next st, 1tr in each of next 2 sts) 3 times, 2tr in next st, 1tr in each of rem 2[3:4] sts, turn. 35[37:39] sts.
Work 1 row straight in tr.
Next row: 2ch, miss st at base of ch, 2tr in next st, 1tr in each st to last 2 sts, 2tr in next st, 1tr in 2nd of 2ch, turn. 37[39:41] sts.
Cont to inc 1 st in this way at each end of every foll 3rd row until there are 51[57:63] sts. Work 5 rows straight. Fasten off.

RIGHT FRONT EDGING:

With 3.50mm (UK 9) hook and RS facing, join A in 1st row of C at lower edge, 1ch, 4dc in row-ends of striped edging, 2dc in each tr row-end to neck, 1dc in top of last tr, turn. Beg each row with 2ch, miss st at base of ch, work 3 rows in dc. Fasten off.

LEFT FRONT EDGING:

Beg at neck edge, work to match Right front edging.

NECKBAND:

Join shoulder seams.

With 3.50mm (UK 9) hook and RS facing, join A in final dc row-end of right front edging, 1ch, 1dc in each of 3 rem dc row-ends, (1dc in each st and 2dc in each tr row-end) around neck, 1dc in each of 4 dc row-ends of left front edging. Fasten off.

1st row: (RS) Join C to 7th st of last row 1ch, 1dc in each st to last 6 sts of last row, turn.

2nd row: 1ch, dc2tog over next 2 sts, 1dc in each st to last 3 sts, dc2tog over next 2 sts, 1dc in last st. Fasten off.

3rd row: (RS) Join B in next A st of neckband, 1ch, dc2tog over next 2 sts, 1dc in each st to last 2 sts, dc2tog over next 2 sts, 1dc in next A st. *** Turn.

4th row: As 2nd.

5th row: Using C instead of B, work as 3rd row to ***, 1dc in next A st, turn.

6th row: 1ch, 1dc in each st, ending 1dc in next A st. Fasten off.

LETTER A:

First piece: With 3.50mm (UK 9) hook and C, make 9ch.

Foundation row: (RS) 1tr in 3rd ch from hook, 1tr in each ch to end, turn. 8 sts.

1st row: 2ch (counts as first tr), miss st at base of ch, 1tr in each st to end, working last tr in 2nd of 2ch, turn.

2nd row: Ss in each of first 2 sts, 2ch, miss st at base of ch, 1tr in each of next 3 sts, turn. 4 sts.** Fasten off.

Second piece: As first piece to **, do not fasten off. Note that from now on some rows beg with 2ch and others with 3ch.

Join: 3rd row: (WS) 3ch, tr2tog over next 2 sts, 2tr in next st, 5ch, with WS of first piece facing, 2tr in first st, tr2tog over next 2 sts, 1tr in 2nd of 2ch, turn. 13 sts.

4th row: 3ch, miss st at base of ch, tr2tog over next 2 sts, 1tr in next st, 1tr in each of 5ch, 1tr in next st, tr2tog over next 2 sts, 1tr in turning ch, turn. 11 sts.

5th row: Beg with 2ch, work in tr.

First side: 6th row: 3ch, miss st at base of ch, 1tr in each of next 3 sts, turn. 4 sts.

7th row: As 5th row.

8th row: 3ch, miss st at base of ch, tr2tog over next 2 sts, 2tr in next st. 4 sts. Fasten off.

Second side: 6th row: (RS) Miss centre 3 sts, rejoin yarn in next st, 2ch, 1tr in each st, turn. 4 sts.

7th row: As 5th row.

8th row: 2ch, 1tr in st at base of ch, tr2tog over next 2 sts, 1tr in last st. 4 sts. Do not fasten off.

Join: 9th row: (WS) 3ch, miss st at base of ch, 1tr in each of next 3 sts of this side, 1tr in each of 4 sts of other side, turn. 8 sts.

10th row: 3ch, miss st at base of ch, tr2tog over next 2 sts, 1tr in each of next 2 sts, tr2tog over next 2 sts, 1tr in last st. 6 sts. Fasten off.

Edgings:

With 3.00mm (UK 11) hook, B and RS facing, work 1 round of dc around outside, making 2dc in each row-end and 3dc in outer corners, join with a ss in first st. Fasten off. Work inside edge to match.

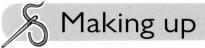 **Making up**

Pin out letter A and damp press. Press rem pieces of jacket according to directions on ball band. Pin letter A in place and stitch, using B split in half to work in backstitch below ch edge of each dc. Use sewing thread to sew snap fasteners to front edgings. Sew a button over each fastener on RS of work. Sew in sleeves, sewing row-ends of last 4 rows of sleeves to armhole shaping. Join side and sleeve seams.

Bound baby blanket

Match fabric and yarn to make a unique personalised baby gift.

Soft and striped in a simple stitch pattern, this cosy blanket has heart motifs appliquéd onto the centre panel and is backed and bound with a coordinating printed fabric.

The Yarn

Sirdar Snuggly Baby Bamboo DK (approx. 95m/104 yards per 50g/1¾oz ball) is a blend of 80% bamboo viscose and 20% wool. It is a practical, easy-care yarn for babies that feels soft and cosy. There is a large palette of colours to choose from.

GETTING STARTED

★★ *Only minimal shaping required on heart motifs but care is needed with sewing fabric finishing touches.*

Size:
Finished size is approximately 70 x 62cm (28 x 24½in)

How much yarn:
4 x 50g (1¾oz) balls of Sirdar Snuggly Baby Bamboo DK in colour A – cream (shade 131)
2 balls in each of colour B – pink (shade 134) and colour C – putty (shade 132)

Hook:
3.50mm (UK 9) crochet hook

Additional items:
80cm (31in) of 140cm (55in) -wide cotton fabric for binding and backing
Matching sewing thread and needle

Tension:
19 sts and 10 rows measure 10cm (4in) square over patt on 3.50mm (UK 9) hook
IT IS ESSENTIAL TO WORK TO THE STATED TENSION TO ACHIEVE SUCCESS

What you have to do:
Work centre panel horizontally and side panels vertically onto centre panel. Work throughout in V stitch and treble group pattern and stripes. Make heart motifs and sew to centre panel. Sew fabric backing onto blanket and bind edges in same fabric.

Instructions

Abbreviations:

ch = chain(s)
cm = centimetre(s)
cont = continue
dc = double crochet
foll = follows
gr = group
patt = pattern
rep = repeat
RS = right side
ss = slip stitch
st(s) = stitch(es)
tr = treble
WS = wrong side

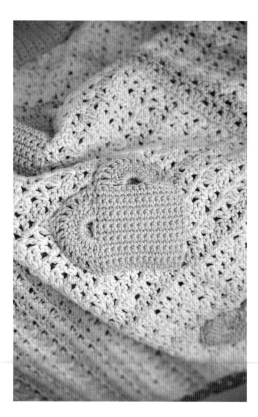

CENTRE PANEL:

With 3.50mm (UK 9) hook and A, make 49ch.

Foundation row: (RS) 1tr into 5th ch from hook, 1ch, 1tr into same ch as last tr, *miss 2ch, 3tr into next ch, miss 2ch, (1tr, 1ch, 1tr – called V st) into next ch, rep from * to last 2ch, miss 1ch, 1tr into last ch, turn.

Patt row: 3ch (counts as first tr), *(1tr, 1ch, 1tr) into centre of next V st, 3tr into centre tr of next 3tr gr, rep from * to last V st, (1tr, 1ch, 1tr) into last V st, 1tr into top of turning ch, turn.

Rep last row twice more. Cont in stripe patt as foll, cutting off A at end of each set of 4 rows, but carrying B up side of work from one stripe to next:

**With B, work 1 row, with A, work 4 rows, rep from ** 11 times more. Fasten off.

RIGHT SIDE PANEL:

With 3.50mm (UK 9) hook and RS of work facing, join B to bottom right-hand corner of Centre panel.

Next row: 1ch (does not count as a st), now work (1dc between 2 edge sts and 1dc into top of end st) in each row to top, working over any loose ends to secure them, turn. 128dc.

Next row: 1ch, 1dc into each dc to end, turn.

Change to C.

Next row: 3ch, *miss 2dc, 3tr into next dc, miss 2dc, (1tr, 1ch, 1tr) into next dc, rep from * to last 2dc, miss 1dc, 1tr into last dc, turn.

Foundation row: (RS) 1dc into 2nd ch from hook, 1dc into each ch to end, turn.
1st row: 1ch (does not count as a st), 1dc into each dc to end, turn. 14dc.
Work 12 more rows in dc.
Shape curves:
Next row: Ss into each of first 6dc, 5ch, miss next 2dc, ss into each of next 3dc, turn.
Next row: 12tr into 5ch loop, miss first 3ss, ss into each of last 3ss, turn.
Next row: (1tr into next tr, 1ch) 11 times, 1tr into last tr, ss into last dc.
Working along adjacent side, cont as foll:
Next row: Miss first row-end, ss into each of next 6 row-ends, 5ch, miss 2 row-ends, ss into each of next 3 row-ends, turn.
Next row: 12tr into 5ch loop, miss first 3ss, ss into each of last 3ss, turn.
Next row: (1tr into next tr, 1ch) 11 times, 1tr into last tr, ss into corner. Fasten off.

1st patt row: 3ch, *(1tr, 1ch, 1tr) into centre of next V st, 3tr into centre tr of next 3tr gr, rep from * to end, 1tr into turning ch, turn.
Change to A.
2nd patt row: 3ch, *3tr into centre tr of next 3tr gr, (1tr, 1ch, 1tr) into centre of next Vst, rep from * to end, 1tr into turning ch, turn.
Rep 1st patt row.
Rep these 2 patt rows, AT SAME TIME working in stripes of 2 rows each B, C and A until 9 stripes have been worked in total. Fasten off.

LEFT SIDE PANEL:
With 3.50mm (UK 9) hook and RS of work facing, join B to top left-hand corner of Centre panel.
Next row: 1ch, now work 128dc evenly along side of Centre panel as before, turn.
Next row: 1ch, 1dc into each dc to end, turn.
Change to C.
Next row: 3ch, *miss 2dc, (1tr, 1ch, 1tr) into next dc, miss 2dc, 3tr into next dc, rep from * to last 2dc, miss 1dc, 1tr into last dc, turn.
Cont in patt as now set, complete to match Right side panel.

HEART MOTIFS: (make 4)
With 3.50mm (UK 9) hook and C, make 15ch.

✂ Making up

Sew 4 hearts to centre panel, positioning them centrally and between 2 stripe repeats.
Cut a 60 x 68cm (24 x 27in) piece of fabric from width of fabric, leaving 20cm (8in) for making binding strips.
With WS facing, tack fabric in place around outer edges of blanket. Work a line of running stitches along second dc row at start of each side panel and around each heart motif to secure to the backing fabric.
Cut 2 strips the full width of fabric x 6cm (2⅜in) wide. Join short ends to make one long strip. With WS facing, fold strip in half lengthwise and press to create a crisp fold. With RS of blanket uppermost and starting at centre of lower edge, sew the binding fabric strip around the outer edges of the blanket, taking a 1cm (½in) seam allowance and making a small pleat in each corner to form a mitre. Fold binding over edge of blanket and slip stitch in place on WS.

Animal egg cosies

Crochet this cute menagerie for the family breakfast table.

Keep your breakfast eggs warm with this cute collection of animal cosies worked in double crochet with simple embroidered features.

 Instructions

DOG COSY:

Note: In 6th–12th rounds, when changing colour, complete last part of last st in new colour and when changing from A to B, work over strand of A to carry it across work to where it is required again. Work throughout with WS facing and turn each section to RS after fastening off.

Body:

*With 4.00mm (UK 8) hook and A, make a magic circle as foll: Wind A several times around tip of left forefinger. Carefully slip ring off finger; insert hook into ring, pull yarn through. Make 1 ch, then work 7dc into ring, join with a ss in first dc. Pull end of yarn gently to close ring. 7 sts.

Marking beg of each round, cont as foll:

1st round: 2dc in each st to end. 14 sts.

2nd round: (2dc in next st, 1dc in next st) 7 times. 21 sts.

3rd round: (2dc in next st, 1dc in each of next 2 sts) 7 times. 28 sts.

GETTING STARTED

★ ★ *Basic fabric and simple shaping but care is needed with details for a good result.*

Size:

Each cosy, when flat, measures approximately 8cm (3in) across x 8cm (3in) tall

How much yarn:

1 x 50g (1¾oz) ball of Rowan Pure Wool DK in each of six colours: A – Mimosa (shade 045); B – Earth (shade 018); C – Gilt (shade 032); D – Snow (shade 012); E – Tea Rose (shade 025); F – Shale (shade 002) Scraps of Black (shade 004) for facial features

Hook:

4.00mm (UK 8) crochet hook

Additional items:

Black sewing thread and needle
8 x 5mm (¼in) black pearl beads
Scrap of orange felt
2.5cm (1in) white pompom

Tension:

11 sts and 12 rows measure 5cm (2in) square over dc on 4.00mm (UK 8) hook
IT IS ESSENTIAL TO WORK TO THE STATED TENSION TO ACHIEVE SUCCESS

What you have to do:

Work each cosy in continuous rounds of double crochet, shaping as described. Make separate features (ears, tails, wings) and sew on. Sew on beads for eyes and embroider facial features using simple embroidery stitches.

The Yarn

Rowan Pure Wool DK (approx. 125m/136 yards per 50g/1¾oz ball) contains 100% wool in a superwash format, which is ideal for these cosies. There is a wide colour range.

Abbreviations:

beg = beginning
ch = chain(s)
cm = centimetre(s)
cont = continue
dc = double crochet
dc2tog = (insert hook into next st and draw a loop through) twice, yarn round hook and draw through all 3 loops
foll = follows
htr = half treble
ss = slip stitch
st(s) = stitch(es)
tr = treble
WS = wrong side

4th round: 1dc in each st to end.
5th round: (2dc in next st, 1dc in each of next 3 sts) 7 times. 35 sts. *
6th round: Work in dc as foll: 2 B, 32 A, 1 B.
7th round: Work in dc as foll: 2 B, 29 A, 4 B.
8th round: Work in dc as foll: 3 B, 28 A, 4 B.
9th round: Work in dc as foll: 3 B, 29 A, 3 B.
10th round: Work in dc as foll: 2 B, 31 A, 2 B.
11th round: Work in dc as foll: 1 B, 33 A, 1 B.
12th round: Work in dc as foll: 1 B, 34 A.
Cut off B and cont in A only.
13th–18th rounds: Work in dc.
19th round: 1dc in each of next 15 sts (mark last dc for centre back), ss in each st to end. Fasten off.

Ear: (make 2)
With 4.00mm (UK 8) hook and B, make a magic circle as for body, 1ch, 6dc in ring, join with a ss in first dc. Pull end of yarn gently to close ring. 6 sts.
1st round: (2dc in next st, 1dc in next st) 3 times. 9 sts.
2nd round: (2dc in next st, 1dc in each of next 2 sts) 3 times. 12 sts.
3rd and 4th rounds: Work in dc.
5th round: (Dc2tog, 1dc in each of next 4 sts) twice. 10 sts.
6th–8th rounds: Work in dc.
9th round: (Dc2tog, 1dc in each of next 3 sts) twice. 8 sts.

10th round: Work in dc.
11th round: (Dc2tog, 1dc in each of next 2 sts) twice. 6 sts.
Ss in next st, then fasten off leaving a long end.

Tail:
With 4.00mm (UK 8) hook and B, make a magic circle as for body, 1ch, 4dc in ring, join with a ss in first dc.
Pull end of yarn gently to close ring. 4 sts.
1st round: Work in dc.
2nd round: (2dc in next st, 1dc in next st) twice. 6 sts.
3rd–11th rounds: Work in dc.
12th round: (2dc in next st, 1dc in each of next 2 sts) twice. 8 sts.
Ss in next st, then fasten off leaving a long end.

DUCK COSY:
Body:
With C, work as given for Dog cosy from * to *.
6th–17th rounds: Work in dc.
18th round: (Miss next st, 3htr in next st, miss next st, ss in next st) to last 3 sts, miss next st, 3htr in next st, ss in next st. Fasten off.
Wing: (make 2)
With 4.00mm (UK 8) hook and C, make a magic circle as for dog cosy, 1ch, 7dc in ring, join with a ss in first dc.
Pull end of yarn gently to close ring. 7 sts.

1st round: (3tr in next st, ss in next st) twice, turn.
2nd round: (WS) 3ch, 3tr in each of next 2tr, ss in each of next 2tr, 3tr in each of next 2tr, now work into remaining 3dc at start, 2dc in each of next 2dc, ss in last dc. Fasten off leaving a long end.

BUNNY COSY:
Body:
With D, work as given for Dog cosy from * to *.
6th–17th rounds: Work in dc.
18th round: Ss in each st to end. Fasten off.
Ear: (make 2)
With 4.00mm (UK 8) hook and D, make a magic circle as for dog cosy, 1ch, 4dc in ring, join with a ss in first dc. Pull end of yarn gently to close ring. 4 sts.
1st round: (2dc in next st, 1dc in next st) twice. 6 sts.
2nd round: (2dc in next st, 1dc in each of next 2 sts) twice. 8 sts.
3rd round: (2dc in next st, 1dc in each of next 3 sts) twice. 10 sts.
Join in E and at each colour change complete last part of last st in new colour.
4th–10th rounds: In dc work, 3 E, 7 D. Cut off E and cont in D only.
11th round: 1dc in each st to end.
12th round: (Dc2tog, 1dc in each of next 3 sts) twice. 8 sts. Fasten off leaving a long end.

CAT COSY:
Body:
With F, work as given for Dog cosy from * to *.
6th–19th rounds: Work in dc.
20th round: Ss in each st to end. Fasten off.
Ear: (make 2 – one in F and one in D)
With 4.00mm (UK 8) hook make a magic circle as for dog cosy, 1ch, 4dc in ring, join with a ss in first dc. Pull end of yarn gently to close ring. 4 sts.
1st round: (2dc in next st, 1dc in next st) twice. 6 sts.
2nd round: (2dc in next st, 1dc in each of next 2 sts) twice. 8 sts.
3rd round: (2dc in next st, 1dc in next st) 4 times. 12 sts.
4th round: (2dc in next st, 1dc in each of next 3 sts) 3 times. 15 sts. Fasten off leaving a long end.
Tail:
With 4.00mm (UK 8) hook and D, make a magic circle as for dog cosy, 1ch, 4dc in ring, join with a ss in first dc. Pull end of yarn gently to close ring. 4 sts.

1st round: (2dc in next st, 1dc in next st) twice. 6 sts.
2nd and 3rd rounds: Work in dc. Cut off D.
4th–17th rounds: Join in F and work in dc.
18th round: 1tr in each of next 3 sts, 1htr in next st, ss in next st. Fasten off leaving a long end.

✂ Making up

DOG COSY:
Position tail at centre back at base of body and sew in place so that it curves around body. Position ears as shown and sew securely in place. Sew on beads for eyes and embroidery facial details and freckles with black yarn.

DUCK COSY:
Cut 3 x 10cm (4in) strands of C for "fluffy feathers". Fold strands in half and pull folded section through top of head to inside and secure in place. Trim feathers to about 2cm (¾in) and unravel to give a frizzy appearance. Sew last 4dc of 2nd round to sides of body. Sew on beads for eyes. Cut scrap of felt into an ellipse and sew in place for beak.

BUNNY COSY:
Sew pompom at centre back at base of body. Position ears as shown and sew securely in place. Sew on beads for eyes. Embroider nose in E, then split black yarn and use to embroider straight stitch whiskers.

CAT COSY:
Position tail at centre back at base of body and sew in place so that it curves around body. Position ears as shown and sew securely in place. Sew on beads for eyes. Embroider nose (small V shape) in E, then split black yarn and use to embroider nose and mouth (an upside-down Y) and straight stitch whiskers.

Delicious cupcakes!

Have fun making these gorgeous cakes, which look good enough to eat.

Tempt your tastebuds with these scrumptious cupcakes. Each cake is worked in cotton yarn and three sections – case, cake top, icing or cream toppings – that you sew together, stuff with toy filling and embellish with sweet decorations.

The Yarn

Anchor Style Creativa (approx. 70m/76 yards per 50g/1¾oz ball) contains 100% mercerized cotton. It makes a soft, silky fabric with a slight sheen and there is a fabulous shade range. Anchor Style Magicline Dotty is similar with printed colours that form dots on the background.

GETTING STARTED

★★ *Each section of cupcake is straightforward to make but care is needed with sewing up and construction for a neat result.*

Size:
Cakes are approximately 12cm (4½in) tall x 5.5cm (2¼in) across base

How much yarn:
For complete set of four cakes:
1 x 50g (1¾oz) ball of Anchor Style Magicline Dotty in colour A – pink variegated (shade 01502)
1 x 50g (1¾oz) ball of Anchor Style Creativa in each of six colours: B – Dark Brown (shade 00381); C – White (shade 01331); D – Beige (shade 01337); E – Pale Pink (shade 01317); F – Red (shade 01333) and G – Cream (shade 00926)
Oddments of cotton yarn in yellow, purple, orange, turquoise and green

Hooks:
3.50mm (UK 9) crochet hook
4.00mm (UK 8) crochet hook

Additional items:
Polyester toy filling
Four 2.5cm (1in)-diameter cardboard discs
1m (1 yard) of 6mm- (¼in-) wide red organza ribbon

Tension:
Work firm and even sts

What you have to do:
Working mainly in rounds throughout, make cupcake case in ribbed effect pattern. Make cake top, icing effects and decorations as directed. Sew sections together, stuffing cake with toy filling.

 Instructions

BIRTHDAY CUPCAKE: Case:

With 4.00mm (UK 8) hook and A, make a magic circle (see Note on page 66).

1st round: 3ch (counts as first tr), work 14tr in ring, join with a ss in 3rd of 3ch and tighten ring. 15 sts.

2nd round: 3ch, 1tr in st at base of ch, 2tr in each st all round, join with a ss in 3rd of 3ch. 30 sts.

3rd round: 1ch (does not count as a st), ss in each st to end. Change to 3.50mm (UK 9) hook.

4th round: 2ch (counts as first htr), 1htr in each st, join with a ss in 2nd of 2ch. Change to 4.00mm (UK 8) hook.

5th–9th rounds: 2ch, 1rhtrb around next st, *1htr in next st, 1rhtrb around next st, rep from * to end, join with a ss in 2nd of 2ch. Change to 3.50mm (UK 9) hook.

10th round: 2ch, 1htr in st at base of ch, ss in next st, *2htr in next st, ss in next st, rep from * to end. Fasten off.

Cake top: With 4.00mm (UK 8) hook and B, make a magic circle as above.

1st round: 3ch (counts as first tr), work 14tr in ring, join with a ss in 3rd of 3ch and tighten ring. 15 sts.

2nd round: 2ch, 1htr in st at base of ch, 1htr in each of next 2 sts, (2htr in next st, 1htr in each of next 2 sts) to end,

Abbreviations:

beg = beginning

ch = chain(s)

cm = centimetre(s)

dc = double crochet

dc2tog = (insert hook in next st, yrh and draw loop through) twice, yrh and draw through all 3 loops on hook

htr = half treble

htr2tog = (yrh, insert hook in next st and draw loop through) twice, yrh and draw through all 5 loops

rem = remain

rep = repeat

rhtrb = inserting hook from back and from right to left, work 1htr around stem of next st

sp = space

ss = slip stitch

st(s) = stitch(es)

tr = treble

WS = WS

yrh = yarn round hook

Note:

Each section is worked with WS facing

join with a ss in 2nd of 2ch. 20 sts.

3rd round: 3ch, 1tr in st at base of ch, 1tr in next st, (2tr in next st, 1tr in next st) to end, join with a ss in 3rd of 3ch. 30 sts.

4th round: 2ch, 1htr in each st, join with a ss in 2nd of 2ch. Fasten off leaving a long tail.

Icing layer:

With 4.00mm (UK 8) hook and C, make a magic circle as above.

1st round: 1ch (does not count as a st), work 9dc in ring, join with a ss in first dc and tighten ring. 9dc.

2nd round: 2dc in each dc to end, join with a ss in first dc. 18dc.

3rd round: (1dc in next dc, 2dc in next dc) to end, join with a ss in first dc. 27dc.

4th round: Ss in next st, *5ch, 1htr in 3rd ch from hook, 1htr in each of next 2ch, miss next st, ss in next st *, **4ch, 1htr in 2nd ch from hook, 1htr in each of next 2ch, miss next st, ss in next st, miss next st, 1htr in next st, 2htr in each of next 2 sts, 1htr in next st **, miss next st, ss in next st, rep from * to *, ss in next st, 5ch, 1tr in 3rd ch from hook, 1tr in each of next 2ch, miss next 2 sts, ss in next st, rep from ** to **, ss in next st. Fasten off leaving a 40cm (15¾in) tail for sewing icing to cake top. Using scraps of bright colours, sew short straight stitches at random over surface of icing.

Candle holder:

With 4.00mm (UK 8) hook and E, make a small flower as foll:

Beg with a 20cm (8in) tail, make a magic circle as above, (3ch, 1tr, ss) 5 times in ring, tighten ring, 1ch. Fasten off.

Candle:

With 3.50mm (UK 9) hook and C, make a magic circle as above.

1st round: 1ch, work 4dc in ring, join with ss in first dc and tighten ring. Working in continuous rounds, work 4 more rounds (16dc), ss in next dc. Fasten off leaving a long tail.

Sew candle to candle holder, then wind a short length of F around candle and secure.

Flame:

With 3.50mm (UK 9) hook and yellow, make 3ch, 1htr in 3rd ch from hook. Fasten off. Sew flame to top of candle.

LOVEHEART CUPCAKE: Case:

Using B instead of A, work as given for Birthday cupcake cake Case.

Cake top:

Using D instead of B, work as given for Birthday cupcake Cake top.

Frilled cream:

With 4.00mm (UK 8) hook and E, make a magic circle as above.

1st round: 1ch (does not count as a st), work 8dc in ring, join with a ss in first dc and tighten ring. 8dc.

2nd round: 4ch (counts as 1tr, 1ch), 1tr in st at base of ch, (1tr, 1ch) twice in each st to end, join with a ss in 3rd of 4ch.

3rd round: 4ch, (1tr, 1ch) 4 times in first ch sp, (1tr, 1ch) 5 times in each ch sp to end, join with a ss in 3rd of 4ch. Fasten off leaving a 40cm (15¾in) tail.

Loveheart decoration:

With 3.50mm (UK 9) hook and F, make 2ch.

1st row: 2dc in 2nd ch from hook, turn. 2dc.

2nd row: 1ch (does not count as a st), 1dc in first dc, 2dc in last dc, turn. 3dc.

3rd row: 1ch, 2dc in first dc, 1dc in next dc, 2dc in last dc, turn. 5dc.

4th row: 1ch, 2dc in first dc, 1dc in each of next 4dc, turn. 6dc.

5th row: 1ch, 2dc in first dc, 1dc in each of next 4dc, 2dc in last dc, turn. 8dc.

6th row: (WS) (1htr, 1tr, 1dtr, 1tr, 1htr) in 2nd dc, ss in each of next 2dc, miss next dc, (1htr, 1tr, 1dtr, 1tr, 1htr) in next dc, miss next dc, ss in last dc, do not turn.

Edging:

Ss round both side edges of heart (working 1dc in pointed tip).

Fasten off leaving a long end.

SMARTIES CUPCAKE: Case:

Using D instead of A, work as given for Birthday cupcake Case.

Cake top:

Using B, work as given for Birthday cupcake Case top.

Base cream swirl:

With 4.00mm (UK 8) hook and C, make 15ch, join with a ss in first ch to form a ring.

1st round: 3ch (counts as first tr), work 29tr in ring, join with a ss in 3rd of 3ch. 30 sts.

2nd round: 2ch (counts as first htr), 1htr in each st to end, join with a ss in 2nd of 2ch.

3rd round: 2ch, (htr2tog over next 2 sts) to last st, htr2tog inserting hook in last st and in 2nd of 2ch. Fasten off.

Middle cream swirl:

Work in same way as Base cream swirl, making 12ch for ring and working 23tr in 1st round.

Top cream swirl:

Work 3 rounds in same way as Base cream swirl, making 9ch for ring and working 17tr in 1st round. 9 sts rem. Do not fasten off.

4th round: 2ch, htr2tog over next 2 sts, (1htr in next st, htr2tog over next 2 sts) twice, join with a ss in 2nd of 2ch. 6 sts.

5th round: (Dc2tog over next 2 sts) 3 times, join with a ss in top of first dc2tog. Fasten off leaving a long end. Thread yarn end back to starting ring, ready for sewing.

Smarties: (make several in bright colours)

With 3.50mm (UK 9) hook, make a magic circle as above.

1st round: 1ch, work 4dc in centre of ring, tighten ring, then join with a ss in first dc, 1ch. Fasten off leaving a long end.

CHERRY CUPCAKE: Case:

Using C instead of A, work as given for Birthday cupcake Case, working last (10th) round in F.

Cake top:

With B, work as given for Birthday cupcake Cake top.

Base cream swirl:

Using G instead of C, work as given for Smarties cupcake Base cream swirl.

Middle cream swirl:

Work in same way as Base cream swirl, making 13ch for ring and working 25tr in 1st round.

Top cream swirl:

Work 3 rounds in same way as Base cream swirl, making 11ch for ring and working 21tr in 1st round. 11 sts rem.

4th round: 2ch, (htr2tog) to end, join with a ss in 2nd of 2ch. Fasten off leaving a long end. Thread yarn end back to starting ring, ready for sewing.

Cherry:

With 4.00mm (UK 8) hook and F, make a magic circle as above.

1st round: 1ch (does not count as a st), work 6dc in ring, join with a ss in first dc and tighten ring. 6dc.

2nd round: 2dc in each dc to end. 12dc.

3rd and 4th rounds: 1dc in each dc to end.

5th round: (1dc in next st, dc2tog over next 2dc) to end. 8dc.

6th round: Stuff cherry firmly with toy filling, then work (dc2tog over next 2 sts) to end. Fasten off leaving a long end.

Stalk: Cut a 13cm (5in) length of B, twist tightly to make a twisted cord (yarn folds back on itself). Knot at frayed end. Using end of cherry yarn, sew stalk into top of cherry.

Making up

BIRTHDAY CUPCAKE:

Insert cardboard disc in base of cupcake case. Fill case loosely with toy filling. Sew cake top to inside of base, just behind sts of frilled edging and leaving a gap to add more filling. Add more filling for a firm, realistic effect, pushing filling under cake top as well. Close gap.* Position icing layer centrally over cake top and sew in place. Sew candle to centre of icing.

LOVEHEART CUPCAKE:

Work as given for Birthday cupcake to *. Arrange frilled cream into a double-layered loop to sit on cake top and secure to cake top with neat stitching. Sew loveheart to centre of frilled cream, setting it on its side and attaching one edge only to frill. Adjust loveheart to stand upright.

SMARTIES CUPCAKE:

Work as given for Birthday cupcake to *. With last round uppermost, position each swirl centrally over previous one and sew together. Arrange smarties evenly over all three swirls and sew in place. Sew cream swirls onto centre of cake top.

CHERRY CUPCAKE:

Work as given for Birthday cupcake to *. Thread organza ribbon through 'ribs' of pattern about 1cm (½in) down from top edge and tie in a bow. With last round uppermost, position each swirl centrally over previous one and sew together. Sew cherry in place in natural dip of top cream swirl. Sew cream swirls onto centre of cake top.

Baby's hooded jacket

It's designer style from day one with this great little jacket.

With its two-tone striped pattern, drop shoulders and buttoned front, this stylish baby's hooded jacket is bound to be a winner.

GETTING STARTED

★★★ *Working stripes and keeping pattern correct when shaping requires concentration.*

Size:
To fit chest: 46–51[56–61]cm (18–20[22–24]in)
Actual size: 59[67]cm (23¼[26½]in)
Length: 32[35.5]cm (12½[14]in)
Sleeve seam: 22[25.5]cm [8½[10]in)
Note: Figures in square brackets [ ] refer to larger size; where there is only one set of figures, it applies to both sizes

How much yarn:
2[3] x 50g (1¾oz) balls of Sirdar Snuggly DK in each of A – Denim Blue (shade 326) and B – Sky Blue (shade 216)

Hook:
4.00mm (UK 8) crochet hook

Additional items:
5 buttons
Safety-pin and marker

Tension:
20.5 sts and 12 rows measure 10cm (4in) square over patt on 4.00mm (UK 8) hook
IT IS ESSENTIAL TO WORK TO THE STATED TENSION TO ACHIEVE SUCCESS

What you have to do:
Work back and fronts in one piece until dividing for armholes. Work throughout in two-row stripes of two toning colours and stitch pattern as described. Work double crochet edgings throughout. Make a tassel for back of hood.

The Yarn

Sirdar Snuggly DK (approx. 165m/180 yards per 50g/1¾oz ball) contains 55% nylon and 45% acrylic. It is a soft, easy-care yarn that is ideal to use for making baby garments. The shade range contains baby pastel colours as well as many bright and deep colours.

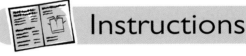 Instructions

BACK AND FRONTS:
(Worked in one piece to armholes) With 4.00mm (UK 8) hook and A, make 111[127]ch.
Foundation row: (WS) 1dc in 2nd ch from hook, 1dc in each ch to end, turn.
Next row: 1ch (does not count as a st), 1dc in each dc to end, turn. 110[126] sts.
Join in B and work 2 more rows in dc.
Change to A and work 1 row.
Inc row: (RS) With A, 1ch, 1dc in each of next 12[14]dc, (2dc in next dc, 1dc in each of next 13[15]dc) 7 times, turn. 117[133]dc.
Working in stripes of 2 rows each B and A, cont in patt as foll:
1st patt row: (WS) 1ch, 1dc in first dc, *1ch, miss 1dc, 1dc in next dc, rep from * to end, turn.
2nd patt row: 3ch, 1tr in first ch sp (counts as first tr2tog), *1ch, tr2tog inserting hook in same sp as previous st for 1st leg and in next sp for 2nd leg, rep from * to last sp, 1ch, tr2tog over last sp and last dc, turn.
3rd patt row: 1ch, 1dc in first st, *1dc in next ch sp, 1ch, miss next tr2tog, rep from * ending with 1dc in last sp, 1dc in last st, turn.
4th patt row: 3ch (counts as first tr), tr2tog inserting

Abbreviations:

beg = beginning
ch = chain(s)
cm = centimetre(s)
cont = continu(e)(ing)
dc = double crochet
foll = follows
inc = increase(d)
patt = pattern
rep = repeat
RS = right side
sp(s) = space(s)
ss = slip stitch
st(s) = stitch(es)
tr = treble
tr2tog = (yrh, insert hook as directed, yrh and draw through a loop, yrh and draw through first two loops on hook) twice, yrh and draw through all 3 loops on hook
WS = wrong side
yrh = yarn round hook

hook in dc at base of 3ch for 1st leg and into first sp for 2nd leg, *1ch, tr2tog inserting hook in same sp as previous st for 1st leg and in next sp for 2nd leg, rep from * working 2nd leg of last tr2tog in last st, 1tr in same st, turn.

5th patt row: 1ch, 1dc in first st, *1ch, miss next tr2tog, 1dc in next sp, rep from * working last dc in 3rd of 3ch, turn.
The 2nd–5th patt rows form patt. Work them 3[4] times more. A total of 8[10] stripes completed and 1st row of next stripe in B.

Divide for armholes:
Right front:
Next row: (RS) With B, 3ch, 1tr in first ch sp, (1ch, tr2tog over 2 sps) 13[15] times, turn.
Beg with 3rd patt row, patt 10 rows, ending with a 4th patt row.

Shape neck:
Next row: With B, 1ch, 1dc in first st, (1ch, miss next tr2tog, 1dc in next sp) 10[12] times, turn.
Next row: With B, ss into next ch sp, dc and foll ch sp, 3ch, tr2tog working 1st leg in sp at base of 3ch, 1ch, patt to end, turn.
Next row: 1ch, 1dc in first st, 1dc in first sp, (1ch, miss tr2tog, 1dc in sp) 7[9] times, turn.
Next row: 3ch, tr2tog over 1st and 2nd sps, patt to end, turn.
Next row: As 5th patt row, ending 1dc in last sp, 1ch, 1dc in 3rd of 3ch, turn.
Next row: 3ch, tr2tog over 1st and 2nd sps, patt to end.
Next row: As 3rd patt row, ending 1dc in last sp, 1ch, 1dc in 3rd of 3ch. Fasten off.

Back:
With RS facing, rejoin B to next sp on last row before dividing for armholes, 3ch, 1tr in next sp, (1ch, tr2tog over 2 sps) 28[32] times, turn.
Beg with 3rd patt row, cont in patt until Back measures same as Right front to shoulder, ending with same patt row. Fasten off.

Left front:
With RS facing, rejoin B to next sp on last row before dividing for armholes, 3ch, 1tr in next sp, (1ch, tr2tog over 2 sps) 13[15] times, working 2nd leg of last rep in last dc, turn.
Beg with 3rd patt row, patt 10 rows, ending with a 4th patt row. Fasten off A and B.

Shape neck:
Next row: With WS facing rejoin B to 3rd sp, 1ch, 1dc in same sp as join, patt to end, turn.
Next row: 3ch, 1tr in first sp, working 1st leg of first tr2tog in same place as last tr work (1ch, tr2tog over 2 sps) 8[10] times, turn.
Next row: With WS facing rejoin A to first sp, 1ch, 1dc in same sp, patt to end, turn.
Next row: Patt until 7th[9th] tr2tog has been worked, 1tr in last dc, turn.

Next row: As 5th patt row.

Next row: Patt to end working last tr2tog over last 2 sps, 1tr in last dc, turn.

Next row: 1ch, 1dc in first tr, (1ch, miss tr2tog, 1dc in sp) 6[8] times, 1dc in 3rd of 3ch. Fasten off.

SLEEVES: (make 2)

With 4.00mm (UK 8) hook and A, make 29ch. Work foundation row as given for Back and fronts. 28 sts. Cont in 2-row stripes of A and B, work 4 rows in dc.

Inc row: 1ch, 1dc in first dc, *2dc in next dc, 1dc in each of next 2dc, rep from * to end, turn. 37dc.

Cont in stripes of 2 rows each B and A. Work 1st patt row as given for Back and fronts.

1st inc row: (RS) 4ch, 1tr in first sp, 1ch, working 1st leg of first tr2tog in same sp as last tr, patt to end working last tr2tog over last sp and last dc, 1tr in last dc, turn.

2nd inc row: 1ch, 1dc in first tr, (1ch, miss tr2tog, 1dc in sp) to end, ending 1dc in last sp, 1ch, 1dc in 4th of 4ch, turn. 2 sts inc over last 2 rows.

Rep these 2 rows 9 times more. 57 sts.

Work 1st inc row once more.

2nd size only: Patt 4 rows.

Both sizes: Fasten off.

LEFT FRONT EDGING:

With 4.00mm (UK 8) hook, A and RS of work facing, work 45[49]dc evenly along Left front edge, turn. Work 1 more row of dc in A. Change to B.

Buttonhole row: With B, 1ch, 1dc in first dc, (2ch, miss next 2dc, 1dc in each of next 8[9]dc) 4 times, 2ch, miss next 2dc, 1dc in each of last 2dc, turn.

Work 1 more row in B, working 2dc in each 2ch sp. Fasten off.

RIGHT FRONT EDGING:

Work as given for Left front edging, omitting buttonholes. Do not fasten off after 2nd row in B; place working loop on a safety-pin.

HOOD:

Join shoulder seams and mark centre back neck.

Right side:

With 4.00mm (UK 8) hook, A and RS of work facing, work 3dc across top of right front edging and 30[32] dc around right front neck to centre back marker, turn. 35[37]dc. Work 3 rows in patt as given for Back and fronts.

Cont in stripes of 2 rows each A and B.

Next row: 1ch, 1dc in each of first 2dc, (1ch, miss 1dc, 1dc in next dc) 16[17] times, 1dc in last dc, turn.

Work 4th and 5th patt rows as given for Back and fronts**.

1st inc row: As 2nd patt row, ending 1tr in turning ch, turn. 1tr inc at end of row.

2nd inc row: 1ch, 1dc in first tr, 1ch, miss tr2tog, 1dc in sp, patt to end as 3rd patt row, turn.

3rd inc row: As 4th patt row, ending 1tr in turning ch, turn. 1tr inc at end of row.

4th inc row: 1ch, 1dc in first tr, 1ch, miss tr2tog, 1dc in sp, patt to end as 5th patt row, turn.

Rep 1st-4th inc rows 5 times more. 47[49] sts. Fasten off.

Left side:

Work to match Right side to **.

1st inc row: 3ch (counts as first tr), tr2tog over first dc and first sp, 1ch, patt to end as 2nd patt row, turn. 1st inc at beg of row.

2nd inc row: As 3rd patt row, ending 1dc in last sp, 1ch, miss tr2tog, 1dc in 3rd of 3ch, turn.

3rd inc row: 3ch, tr2tog over first dc and first sp, 1ch, patt to end as 4th patt row, turn. 1st inc at beg of row.

4th inc row: As 5th patt row, ending 1dc in last sp, 1ch, miss tr2tog, 1dc in 3rd of 3ch, turn.

Rep 1st-4th inc rows 5 times more. 47[49] sts. Fasten off.

Join hood centre back and top seam.

Hood edging:

Return to loop left on safety-pin on Right front edging and, with A, work in dc as set up Right front edging to neck edge and then evenly around outer edge of hood and down Left front edging to lower edge. Work 1 row in dc. Fasten off.

✂ Making up

Join sleeve seams. Sew in sleeves. Sew on buttons. Using A, make a small tassel and sew to back point of hood.

Cheffy pig amigurumi

This little pig makes a good foody friend for your child

This irresistible little piggy in his chef's whites is worked in easy double crochet with embroidered details.

The Yarn

Patons Fab DK (approx. 68m/74 yards per 25g/1oz ball) contains 100% acrylic. Available in lots of colours, the small-size balls are perfect for craft projects and it is machine-washable.

Instructions

Notes:

With exception of ears, all pieces are worked with WS facing. Turn to RS before stuffing. When fastening off each piece, leave a long tail to use for sewing up. When working Body in two colours, introduce new colour on last part of last st in old colour and work over yarn not in use to carry it to its next position.

HEAD:

With 4.00mm (UK 8) hook and A, make a magic circle (see Note on page 66).

1st round: 1ch, work 6dc in ring, join with a ss in first dc, pull end of yarn gently to close circle. 6dc.

Work in a continuous spiral, using a st marker to mark beg of each round.

2nd round: 2dc in each dc to end. 12dc.

3rd round: (2dc in next dc, 1dc in foll dc) to end. 18dc.

4th round: (2dc in next dc, 1dc in each of foll 2dc) to end. 24dc.

5th round: (2dc in next dc, 1dc in each of foll 3dc) to end. 30dc.

6th round: 1dc in each dc to end.

7th round: (2dc in next dc, 1dc in each of foll 4dc) to end. 36dc.

Abbreviations:

beg = beginning
ch = chain(s)
cm = centimetre(s)
cont = continue
dc = double crochet
dc2tog = (insert hook in next st, yrh and draw a loop through) twice, yrh and draw through all 3 loops
foll = follow(s)(ing)
htr = half treble
inc = increased
ss = slip stitch
st(s) = stitch(es)
tr = treble
tr5tog = (yrh, insert hook in next st, yrh and draw a loop through, yrh and draw through first 2 loops) 5 times, yrh and draw through all 6 loops
WS = wrong side
yrh = yarn round hook

8th–11th rounds: Work 4 rounds in dc.
12th round: (Dc2tog, 1dc in each of next 4dc) to end. 30dc.
13th round: (Dc2tog, 1dc in each of next 3dc) to end. 24dc.
14th round: (Dc2tog, 1dc in each of next 2dc) to end. 18dc.
15th round: (Dc2tog, 1dc in next dc) to end. 12dc. Fasten off.
Stuff head firmly with toy filling.

Ears: (make 2)

With 4.00mm (UK 8) hook and A, make a magic circle as above.
1st round: 1ch, work 5dc in ring, join with a ss in first dc, pull end of yarn gently to close circle. 5dc.
2nd round: 1dc in each dc to end.
3rd round: 2dc in each dc to end. 10dc.
4th round: As 3rd round of Head. 15dc. Fasten off.

Snout:

With 4.00mm (UK 8) hook and A, make a magic circle as above.

1st round: 1ch, work 9dc in ring, join with a ss in first dc, pull end of yarn gently to close circle. 9dc.
2nd round: 1dc in each dc to end.
3rd round: 1dc in front loop only of each dc to end, ss in next dc. Fasten off.

BODY:

Work as given for Head to completion of 3rd round.
4th round: *With B, 2dc in next dc, 1dc in each of foll 2dc, with A, (2dc in next dc, 1dc in each of foll 2dc) twice, rep from * once more. 24 sts.
5th round: *With B, 2dc in next dc, 1dc in each of foll 3dc, with A, (2dc in next dc, 1dc in each of foll 3dc) twice, rep from * once more. 30 sts.
6th round: (Note: there are colour changes within inc sts) With B, 2dc in next dc, with A, 1dc in each of foll 3dc, with B, 1dc in next dc, with B, then A, 2dc in next dc, with A, 1dc in each of foll 4dc, 2dc in next dc, 1dc in each of foll 3dc, with B, 1dc in next dc, with B, then A, 2dc in next dc, with A, 1dc in each of foll 3dc, with B, 1dc in next dc, with B, then A, 2dc in next dc, with A, 1dc in each of foll 4dc, with B, 1dc in last dc. 36 sts.
7th round: (Note: there are colour changes within inc sts) With B, then A, 2dc in next dc, with A, 1dc in each of foll 5dc, with B, 2dc in next dc, with A, 1dc in each of foll 5dc, 2dc in next dc, 1dc in each of foll 3dc, with B, 1dc in each of foll 2dc, with A, 2dc in next dc, 1dc in each of foll 5dc, with B, 2dc in next dc, 1dc in foll dc, with A, 1dc in each of next 4dc, 2dc in foll dc, 1dc into each of next 3dc, with B, 1dc in each of last 2dc. 42 sts.
8th round: Work in dc as foll: 8 A, 2 B, 8 A, 3 B, 8 A, 2 B, 9 A, 2 B.
9th round: With A, 2dc in next dc, 1dc in each of foll 6dc, 2dc in next dc, with B, 1dc in each of foll 2dc, with A, 1dc in each of next 4dc, 2dc in foll dc, 1dc in next dc, with B, 1dc in each of foll 2dc, with A, 1dc in each of next 3dc, 2dc in foll dc, 1dc in

each of next 5dc, with B, 1dc in foll dc, 2dc in next dc, with A, 1dc in each of foll 6dc, 2dc in next dc, 1dc in each of foll 2dc, with B, 1dc in each of next 2dc, with A, 1dc in each of last 2dc. 48 sts.

10th round: Work in dc as foll: 8 A, 2 B, 9 A, 2 B, 10 A, 16 B, 1 A.

11th round: Work in dc as foll: 7 A, 3 B, 9 A, 3 B, 8 A, 18 B.

12th round: Work in dc as foll: 10 B, 7 A, 31 B. Fasten off A.

13th–15th rounds: With B only, work 3 rounds in dc.

16th round: (Dc2tog, 1dc in each of next 6dc) to end. 42 sts.

17th round: Work in dc.

18th round: (Dc2tog, 1dc in each of next 5dc) to end. 36 sts.

19th–22nd rounds: Work as 12th–15th rounds of Head. 12 sts.

Stuff Body firmly with toy filling.

23rd round: (Dc2tog) to end. 6 sts.

24th round: (Dc2tog) to end. 3 sts. Fasten off.

Tail:
With 4.00mm (UK 8) hook and A, make 16ch.

1st row: Miss first ch, 2dc in each ch to end. 30dc. Fasten off.

Apron ties:
With 4.00mm (UK 8) hook and using B double, make 30ch. Fasten off.

Apple appliqué:
With C, work as given for Ears to completion of 1st round. 5dc.

2nd round: 2dc in each dc to last st, 1dc and 1ss in last st. 10 sts. Fasten off.

Leaf:
With 4.00mm (UK 8) hook and D, make 3ch.

1st row: 1dc in 2nd ch from hook, ss in next ch, 1ch. Fasten off.

ARMS: (make 2)
Work as given for Head to completion of 2nd round. 12dc.

3rd and 4th rounds: Work in dc.

5th round: (Dc2tog, 1dc in each of next 4dc) twice. 10 sts.

6th–8th rounds: Work 3 rounds in dc. Fasten off.
Stuff 'hand' part only of Arm with toy filling.

LEGS: (make 2)
Work as given for Head to completion of 2nd round. 12dc.

3rd–7th rounds: Work 5 rounds in dc. Fasten off.
Stuff firmly with toy filling.

HAT:
With B instead of A, work as given for Head to completion of 1st round.

2nd round: 2dc in each dc to end, join with a ss in first dc. 12dc.

3rd round: 3ch (counts as first tr), miss st at base of ch, 5tr in next st, (1tr in next st, 5tr in next st) 5 times, join with a ss in 3rd of 3ch. 36 sts.

4th round: 3ch, miss st at base of ch, tr5tog over next 5tr, (1tr in next st, tr5tog over next 5tr) 5 times, join with a ss in 3rd of 3ch. 12 sts.

5th and 6th rounds: 2ch (counts as first htr), miss st at base of ch, 1htr in each st to end, join with a ss in 2nd of 2ch.

7th round: 1ch, 1dc in back loop only of each st to end, join with a ss in first dc. Fasten off.
Stuff with toy filling.

Making up

With B, chain stitch around outer edges of apron to give a neat line. Sew head firmly to body. Making sure the higher edge of apron is at front of body and using photograph as a guide, attach snout and ears to head. Position each arm directly under apron strap on either side of body and sew in place. Sew legs to lower edge of body, leaving a 1.5cm (⅝in) gap between them.

Sew apple and leaf on front of apron, then use E to embroider stalk. With E, embroider eyes and nostrils and use F to embroider cheeks with cross-hatching.

Sew curly tail in place on back, about halfway between base of body and edge of apron. Sew tie to centre of top edge of apron, forming it into a bow and stitching in place. Sew hat firmly in place on top of head.

Lined baby boots

Bring a designer look to the nursery with these
cute lined boots.

Keep tiny toes cosy in these snug pull-on boots worked in a soft angora-blend yarn. They have a contrast-coloured lined cuff with buttons and stitching details.

GETTING STARTED

★ ★ *Easy stitches but details need attention to achieve a good result.*

Size:

To fit age: 0–3[3–6:6–12] months

Length of foot: about 10[12:13]cm (4[4¾:5]in)

Overall height: about 7.5[8:8.5]cm (3[3¼:3⅜]in)

Note: Figures in square brackets [ ] refer to larger sizes; where there is only one set of figures, it applies to all sizes

How much yarn:

1 x 50g (1¾oz) ball of Orkney Angora St Magnus 50/50 DK in each of colour A – Natural (shade 26) and colour B – Fawn (shade 25)

Hook:

4.00mm (UK 8) crochet hook

Additional item:

4 buttons

Tension:

18 sts and 20 rows measure 10cm (4in) square over dc on 4.00mm (UK 8) hook

IT IS ESSENTIAL TO WORK TO THE STATED TENSION TO ACHIEVE SUCCESS

What you have to do:

Work sole and upper of each boot in rounds of double crochet, shaping as directed. Work ankle sections in rows of mock rib, making a lined section in contrast colour at same time. Crochet lined ankle sections together and then sew onto boot. Embroider stitching details in chain stitch using contrast colour.

The Yarn

Orkney Angora St Magnus 50/50 DK (approx. 200m/218 yards per 50g/1¾oz ball) is a luxurious blend of 50% angora with 50% lambswool. This super-soft yarn is perfect for cosy accessories and is available in 35 superb shades.

Instructions

Abbreviations:

beg = beginning

ch = chain

cm = centimetre(s)

dc = double crochet

dc2tog = (insert hook in next st, yrh and draw a loop through) twice, yrh and draw through all 3 loops on hook

rep = repeat

RS = right side

ss = slip stitch

st(s) = stitch(es)

WS = wrong side

yrh = yarn round hook

RIGHT BOOT:
Sole:
With 4.00mm (UK 8) hook and A, make 12[13:14]ch.

Foundation round: 1dc in 2nd ch from hook, 1dc in each of next 9 [10:11]ch, 5dc in last ch, then working in opposite side of ch work 1dc in each of next 9[10:11]ch, 2dc in same ch as first dc, join with a ss in first dc. 26[28:30] sts.

1st round: 1ch (counts as first dc), 2dc in next dc, 1dc in each of next 9[10:11]dc, 2dc in each of next 5dc, 1dc in each of next 9[10:11] dc, 2dc in last dc, join with a ss in 1ch. 33[35:37] sts.

2nd round: 1ch, miss st at base of ch, 2dc in next dc, 1dc in each of next 11[12:13]dc, 2dc in each of next 3dc, 1dc in each of next 3dc, work 2dc in each of next 2dc, 1dc in each of next 11[12:13] dc, 2dc in last dc, join with a ss in 1ch. 40[42:44] sts.

3rd round: 1ch, miss st at base of ch, 2dc in next dc, 1dc in each of next 12[13:14] dc, 2dc in each of next 11dc, 1dc in each of next 14[15:16]dc, 2dc in last dc, join with a ss in 1ch. 53[55:57] sts.

4th round: 1ch, miss st at base of ch, 2dc in next dc, 1dc in each of next 21[22:23] dc, 2dc in each of next 5dc, 1dc in each of next 25[26:27]dc, change to B, join with a ss in 1ch. 59[61:63] sts.

Upper:
5th round: 1ch, miss st at base of ch, working in back loops only, 1dc in each of next 17[18:19]dc, (dc2tog) 14 times, 1dc in each of next 13[14:15]dc, join with a ss in 1ch. 45[47:49] sts.

6th round: 1ch, miss st at base of ch, 1dc in each dc to end, join with a ss in 1ch.

7th round: 1ch, miss st at base of ch, 1dc in each of next 16[17:18]dc, (dc2tog) 5 times, 1dc in each of next 18[19:20]dc, join with a ss in 1ch. 10[12:11] sts.

8th round: As 6th.

9th round: 1ch, 1dc in each of next

14[15:16]dc, (dc2tog) 5 times, 1dc in each of next 15[16:17]dc, join with a ss in 1ch. 35[37:39] sts.

10th round: 1ch, 1dc in each of next 11[12:13]dc, (dc2tog) 5 times, 1dc in each of next 13[14:15]dc, join with a ss in 1ch. 30[32:34] sts.

11th round: As 6th.

12th round: 1ch, 1dc in each of next 9[10:11]dc, (dc2tog) 5 times, 1dc in each of next 10[11:12]dc, join with a ss in 1ch. 25[27:29] sts. Fasten off.

Ankle section: (make 1 in A and 1 in B)
With 4.00mm (UK 8) hook, make 9[10:11]ch.

Foundation row: 1dc in 2nd ch from hook, 1dc in each ch to end, turn. 8[9:10] sts.

Next row: (WS) 1ch (does not count as a st), 1dc in front loop only of each dc to end, turn.

Next row: (RS) 1ch, 1dc in back loop only of each dc to end, turn.

Rep last 2 rows until strip measures 18[19:20]cm from beg, ending with a WS row.

Buttonhole row: 1ch, working in back loop only, 1dc in each of next 2dc, 1ch, miss 1dc, 1dc in each of next 2[3:4]dc, 1ch, miss 1dc, 1dc in each of last 2dc, turn.
Work 1 more row in dc, working 1dc in each 1ch space. Fasten off.

LEFT BOOT:
Sole:
Work as given for Sole of Right boot to completion of 2nd round.

3rd round: 1ch, miss st at base of ch, 2dc in next dc, 1dc in each of next 14[15:16]dc, 2dc in each of next 11dc, 1dc in each of next 12[13:14] dc, 2dc in last dc, join with a ss in 1ch. 53[55:57] sts.

4th round: 1ch, miss st at base of ch, 2dc in next dc, 1dc in each of next 25[26:27]dc, 2dc in each of next 5dc, 1dc in each of next 21[22:23]dc, change to B, join with a ss in 1ch. 59[61:63] sts.

Upper:
5th round: 1ch, miss st at base of ch, working in back loops only, 1dc in each of next 13[14:15]dc, (dc2tog) 14 times, 1dc in each of next 17[18:19]dc, join with a ss in 1ch. 45[47:49] sts.

6th round: 1ch, miss st at base of ch, 1dc in each dc to end, join with a ss in 1ch.

7th round: 1ch, miss st at base of ch, 1dc in each of next 18[19:20]dc, (dc2og) 5 times, 1dc in each of next 16[17:18]dc, join with a ss in 1ch. 40[42:44] sts.

8th round: As 6th.

9th round: 1ch, miss st at base of ch, 1dc in each of next 15[16:17]dc, (dc2tog) 5 times, 1dc in each of next 14[15:16]dc, join with a ss in 1ch. 35[37:39] sts.

10th round: 1ch, miss st at base of ch, 1dc in each of next 13[14:15]dc, (dc2tog) 5 times, 1dc in each of next 11[12:13]dc, join with a ss in 1ch. 30[32:34] sts.

11th round: As 6th.

12th round: 1ch, 1dc in each of next 10[11:12]dc, (dc2tog) 5 times, 1dc in each of next 9[10:11]dc, join with a ss in 1ch. 25[27:29] sts. Fasten off.

Ankle section: (make 1 in A and 1 in B)
Work as given for Right boot.

✂ Making up

Place one A and one B ankle section together with WS facing. With 4.00mm (UK 8) hook, A and RS of section in B facing, work 1dc through edges of both pieces to join. Work along each side, working 2dc in each corner and join with a ss in first dc.

Sew double thickness ankle section to top edge of upper of each boot, overlapping buttonhole edge at outside and leaving overlap unsewn. Sew on buttons to correspond with buttonholes.

With A, embroider chain stitch in an arc up each side and across back heel of each boot.

Book bag and apple cosy

Any child will be the envy of the playground with this
co-ordinated wave-pattern bag set

GETTING STARTED

⭐⭐ *Simple construction but chevron wave pattern requires concentration.*

Size:

Bag: 33cm (13n) tall x 26cm (10¼in) wide x 5cm (2in) deep; handles are 68cm (26¾in) long (when sewn on bag)

Cosy: approximately 11cm (4¼in) wide x 9.5cm (3¾in) tall

How much yarn:

3 x 50g (1¾oz) balls of Rowan Amy Butler Belle Organic DK in colour A – Cornflower (shade 002) 1 ball in each of three other colours: B – Garnet (shade 021); C – Basil (shade 005) and D – Peony (shade 008)

Hook:

4.00mm (UK 8) crochet hook

Additional items:

50cm (⅝ yard) of medium-weight cotton twill fabric to line bag

2 metres (2¼ yards) of 5cm (2in)-wide velvet ribbon to line handles

Sewing needle and thread to match colours A and C

Tension:

2 patt reps measure 8.5cm (3⅜in) and 12 rows measure 9.5cm (3¾in) over patt on 4.00mm (UK 8) hook

IT IS ESSENTIAL TO WORK TO THE STATED TENSION TO ACHIEVE SUCCESS

What you have to do:

Work bag back and front in a chevron wave stitch pattern using four colours. Work double crochet around sides and base of bag to form gussets. Work each handle in double crochet in two sections, join with a contrast colour and line with ribbon. Sew handles on bag and cover each end with a circular motif. Make fabric lining to strengthen bag. Work apple cosy in rounds of same pattern as bag with drawstring closing.

With handles long enough to fit over the shoulder and a gusset to accommodate books and files, this bag in an eye-catching chevron and wave pattern is sure to be popular for school, especially as it has a coordinating circular apple cosy with a drawstring fastening.

The Yarn

Rowan Amy Butler Belle Organic DK (approx. 120m/131 yards per 50g/1¾ oz ball) contains 50% organic wool and 50% organic cotton. Available in a variety of shades, this yarn produces a fabric that is lightweight yet strong.

Instructions

BOOK BAG BACK:

With 4.00mm (UK 8) hook and A, make 38ch loosely.

Foundation row: (RS) 1dc in 2nd ch from hook, 1dc in each ch to end, turn. 37 sts.

1st row: 1ch (does not count as a st), 1dc in first st, *1htr in next st, 1tr in next st. 3dtr in next st, 1tr in next st, 1htr in next st, 1dc in next st, rep from * to end, changing to B on last st, turn. 49 sts.

ch = chain
cm = centimetre(s)
cont = continue
dc = double crochet
dc2(3)tog = (insert hook
in next st, yrh and draw
through a loop) 2(3) times,
yrh and draw through all
3(4) loops on hook
dtr = double treble
dtr2(3)tog = leaving last
loop of each st on hook,
work 1dtr in each of next
2(3) sts, yrh and draw
through all 3(4) loops on
hook
foll = follows
htr = half treble
patt = pattern
rep(s) = repeat(s)
RS = right side
ss = slip stitch
st(s) = stitch(es)
tog = together
tr = treble
WS = wrong side
yrh = yarn round hook

2nd row: With B, 1ch, dc2tog over first 2 sts, 1dc in each of next 2 sts, *3dc in next st, 1dc in each of next 2 sts, dc3tog over next 3 sts, 1dc in each of next 2 sts, rep from * to last 5 sts, 3dc in next st, 1dc in each of next 2 sts, dc2tog over last 2 sts, turn.

3rd row: As 2nd row but changing to C on last st.

4th row: With C, 4ch, miss st at base of ch, 1dtr in next st (counts as first dtr2tog), *1tr in next st, 1htr in next st, 1dc in next st, 1htr in next st, 1tr in next st **, dtr3tog over next 3 sts, rep from *, ending last rep at **, dtr2tog over last 2 sts, turn. 37 sts.

5th row: 1ch, 1dc in each st to end (omitting turning ch), changing to D on last st, turn.

6th row: With D, as 5th row.

These 6 rows form patt. Changing colours every 2 rows in sequence as set, patt a further 35 rows, ending with a 5th patt row in A. Do not turn at end of last row.

Gusset:

With A and RS of work facing, 1ch (does not count as a st), work 49dc evenly spaced along row-ends down one side of bag (7dc from each 6-row patt rep), 1dc in each ch along reverse side of foundation ch and 49dc up other side of bag, turn. 135dc. Work 4 rows in dc. Fasten off.

BOOK BAG FRONT:

Work as given for Back.

HANDLE: (make 4)

With 4.00mm (UK 8) hook and A, make 140ch loosely.

Foundation row: (WS) 1dc in 2nd ch from hook, 1dc in each ch to end, turn. 139 sts.

1st row: 1ch (does not count as a st), 1dc in each st to end, turn.

Rep last row twice more. Fasten off.

CIRCLE: (make 4)

With 4.00mm (UK 8) hook and A, make a magic circle (see Note on page 66).

1st round: 1ch, work 6dc in ring, join with a ss in first dc and pull yarn end up tightly to close circle. 6 sts.

2nd round: 1ch (does not count as a st), 2dc in each st to end, join with a ss in first dc. 12 sts.

3rd round: 1ch, (1dc in next st, 2dc in next st) 6 times, join with a ss in first dc. 18 sts.

4th round: 1ch, (1dc in each of next 2 sts, 2dc in next st) 6 times, join with a ss in first dc, changing to C. 24 sts.

5th round: With C, 1ch, (1dc in each of next 3 sts, 2dc in next st) 6 times, join with a ss in first dc. 30 sts. Fasten off.

Making up

First, use bag back or front as a template for lining fabric and cut out two pieces, allowing 1cm (½in) extra on all sides.

Place bag back and front with WS facing and using C, ss together through back loop of each st around side and lower edges. Place two handles with WS facing and top edges together and, using C, ss together through back loop of each st along top edges. Join remaining two handles in same way. Pin a length of ribbon on WS of each handle for reinforcement and neatly slip stitch in place with sewing thread. Sew ends of handles in place on RS on bag back and front as shown in photograph and cover each end with a circle; neatly slip stitch circles in place with sewing thread.

With RS of bag lining together, join side and base seams, taking 1cm (½in) seam allowances. Then stitch across corners at base to form a gusset same width as bag. Turn 1cm (½in) at top edge of lining to WS and slip lining into bag. Slip stitch lining in place around top edge.

APPLE COSY:

With 4.00mm (UK 8) hook and A only, work as given for Circle until completion of 5th round (30 sts) but do not fasten off.

6th round: 1ch, 1dc in each dc, join with a ss in first dc. Cont in patt as foll:

1st round: 1ch (does not count as a st), 1dc in first st, *1htr in next st, 1tr in next st, 3dtr in next st, 1tr in next st, 1htr in next st, 1dc in next st, rep from * to end, omitting 1dc at end of last rep, change to B and join with a ss in first dc.

2nd round: With B, 1ch, dc2tog over first 2 sts, 1dc in each of next 2 sts, *3dc in next st, 1dc in each of next 2 sts, dc3tog over next 3 sts, 1dc in each of next 2 sts, rep from * to last 4 sts, 3dc in next st, 1dc in next st, dc2tog over last 2 sts, join with a ss in first st.

3rd round: As 2nd round, changing to C to join with a ss in first st.

4th round: With C, 4ch, miss st at base of ch, 1dtr in next st (counts as dtr2tog), *1tr in next st, 1htr in next st, 1dc in next st, 1htr in next st, 1tr in next st, dtr3tog over next 3 sts, rep from * omitting dtr3tog at end of last rep, 1dtr in last st, join with a ss in 4th of 4ch.

5th round: 1ch, 1dc in st at base of ch, miss next dtr, 1dc in each st to last dtr, miss last dtr, change to D and join with a ss in first dc.

Top edging:

Next round: With D, 1ch, (1dc in each of next 3dc, dc2tog) 6 times, join with a ss in first dc. 24 sts. Work 2 rounds in dc.

Eyelet-hole round: 1ch, 1dc in st at base of ch, *1ch, miss next st, 1dc in next st, rep from * to end, 1ch, miss last st, join with a ss in first dc.

Next round: 1ch, 1dc in each st and ch space of previous round, join with a ss in first dc. Fasten off.

Cord:

With 4.00mm (UK 8) hook and A, make 70ch. Fasten off. Thread cord through eyelet holes and knot each end of cord.

Bobbie Bear

This adorable bear is a good first-time toy project since it is worked in easy stitches.

Made in natural colours and soft alpaca yarn, each section of this charming bear is worked mainly in rounds of double crochet and sewn onto the body.

GETTING STARTED

★★ *Easy double crochet fabric but take care with making and stuffing for a good finished result.*

Size:
Bear measures 32cm (12½in) tall

How much yarn:
3 x 50g (1¾oz) balls of King Cole Baby Alpaca in colour A – Fawn (shade 501)
1 ball in colour B – Koala (shade 504)

Hook:
4.00mm (UK 8) crochet hook

Additional items:
Stitch marker
Polyester toy filling

Tension:
First 5 rounds for head measure 5cm (2in) over dc on 4.00mm (UK 8) hook
IT IS ESSENTIAL TO WORK TO THE STATED TENSION TO ACHIEVE SUCCESS

What you have to do:
Make head, body, two arms and two legs in rounds of double crochet, shaping as directed. Stuff all body parts with toy filling. Make nose in contrast colour and sew onto face, adding facial details. Sew all body parts firmly to body.

The Yarn
King Cole Baby Alpaca DK (approx. 100m/109 yards per 50g/1¾oz ball) is a double knitting weight yarn containing 100% baby alpaca. This beautiful yarn produces a soft hand-wash fabric. There is a good selection of both natural and stronger colours.

 Instructions

HEAD:
With 4.00mm (UK 8) hook and A, make a magic circle (see Note on page 66).
1st round: 1ch, work 7dc into ring, join with a ss into first dc and tighten end of yarn to close hole. 7 sts.
Insert marker to denote beg/end of rounds and work in continuous rounds, slipping marker on each round.
2nd round: 2dc into each st to end. 14 sts.
3rd round: (2dc into next st, 1dc into foll st) 7 times. 21 sts.
4th round: (2dc into next st, 1dc into each of foll 2 sts) 7 times. 28 sts.
5th round: (2dc into next st, 1dc into each of foll 3 sts) 7 times. 35 sts.
Cont in this way, inc 7 sts on each round and working 1 more st between incs, until 10th round has been completed and there are 70 sts.
11th–14th rounds: 1dc into each dc to end.
15th round: (Dc2tog, 1dc into each of next 8 sts) 7 times. 63 sts.
16th round: (Dc2tog, 1dc into each of next 7 sts) 7 times. 56 sts.

Abbreviations:

beg = beginning
ch = chain(s)
cm = centimetre(s)
cont = continue
dc = double crochet **dc-2tog** = (insert hook into next st, yrh and draw a loop through) twice, yrh and draw through 3 loops on hook
foll = following
inc(s) = increas(es)(ing)
ss = slip stitch
st(s) = stitch(es)
tr = treble
yrh = yarn round hook

17th round: (Dc2tog, 1dc into each of next 6 sts) 7 times. 49 sts.
18th round: (Dc2tog, 1dc into each of next 5 sts) 7 times. 42 sts.
19th round: (Dc2tog, 1dc into each of next 12 sts) 3 times. 39 sts.
20th round: (Dc2tog, 1dc into each of next 11 sts) 3 times. 36 sts.
21st round: (Dc2tog, 1dc into each of next 4 sts) 6 times. 30 sts.
22nd round: (Dc2tog, 1dc into each of next 4 sts) 5 times. 25 sts.
23rd round: (Dc2tog, 1dc into each of next 3 sts) 5 times. 20 sts.
24th round: (Dc2tog, 1dc into each of next 3 sts) 4 times. 16 sts.
25th round: (Dc2tog, 1dc into each of next 2 sts) 4 times. 12 sts.
Stuff firmly with toy filling.
26th round: (Dc2tog) 6 times. 6 sts.
27th round: (Dc2tog) 3 times. 3 sts.
Fasten off. Cose hole neatly with yarn tail.

BODY:
Work as given for Head to completion of 5th round.

Cont in this way, inc 7 sts on each round and working 1 more st between incs, until 9th round has been completed and there are 63 sts.
10th–18th rounds: 1dc into each dc to end.
19th round: (Dc2tog, 1dc into each of next 7 sts) 7 times. 56 sts.
20th–22nd rounds: 1dc into each dc to end.
23rd round: (Dc2tog, 1dc into each of next 6 sts) 7 times. 49 sts.
24th–27th rounds: 1dc into each dc to end.
28th round: (Dc2tog, 1dc into each of next 5 sts) 7 times. 42 sts.
29th–31st rounds: 1dc into each dc to end.
32nd round: (Dc2tog, 1dc into each of next 4 sts) 7 times. 35 sts.
33rd–37th rounds: 1dc into each dc to end.
38th round: (Dc2tog, 1dc into each of next 5 sts) 5 times. 30 sts.
39th round: 1dc into each dc to end.
Fasten off leaving a long tail.

ARMS: (make 2)

Work as given for Head to completion of 2nd round.

3rd round: 1dc into each dc to end.

4th round: (2dc into next st, 1dc into foll st) 7 times. 21 sts.

5th–16th rounds: 1dc into each dc to end.

17th round: (Dc2tog, 1dc into each of next 5 sts) 3 times. 18 sts.

18th round: 1dc into each dc to end.

19th round: (Dc2tog) 9 times. 9 sts. Fasten off leaving a long tail.

LEGS: (make 2)

Work as given for Head to completion of 4th round.

5th round: 1dc into each dc to end.

6th round: (2dc into next st, 1dc into each of foll 3 sts) 7 times. 35 sts.

7th round: 1dc into each dc to end.

8th round: (Dc2tog, 1dc into each of next 3 sts) 7 times. 28 sts.

9th–12th rounds: 1dc into each dc to end.

13th round: (Dc2tog, 1dc into each of next 2 sts) 7 times. 21 sts.

14th–20th rounds: 1dc into each dc to end. Fasten off leaving a long tail.

EARS: (make 2)

Work as given for Head to completion of 4th round.

5th round: 1dc into each dc to end. Fasten off leaving a long tail.

Fold ear in half and whip st around curved edge of semi-circle.

NOSE:

With B instead of A, work as given for Head to completion of 3rd round.

4th round: 1tr into each of first 4 sts, 1dc into each of next 5 sts, 1tr into each of foll 4 sts, 1dc into each of last 8 sts, ss into next st. Fasten off leaving a long tail.

Making up

Stuff body, arms and legs firmly.

Sew features on face, positioning nose over finishing end of head, and working two curved backstitch eyes and a straight st beneath nose with B. Pin straight edge of ears in position on top of head and sew in place.

Pin head to body and sew securely in place. Pin arms and legs in position, using picture as a guide, and sew securely in place.

Motif mobile

Inspire a lifelong love of crochet in the cradle with this
unique mobile of many different shapes and colours.

Suspended from a crochet-covered metal ring, this mobile is a mass of motifs in different shapes and a variety of pretty colours.

The Yarn

Rowan Siena 4 Ply (approx. 140m/153 yards per 50g/1¾ oz ball) is an 100% mercerized cotton yarn. It produces a fabric with a tight twist and matt sheen, which is ideal for craft projects. There is a wide colour range.

GETTING STARTED

★ ★ *Motifs are easy to make but care is needed with assembly of mobile.*

Size:

Motifs vary in size from approximately 6–9cm (2¼–3½in) in diameter

How much yarn:

1 x 50g (1¾oz) ball of Rowan Siena 4 ply in each of five colours: Greengage (green – shade 661); Madras (mustard – shade 675); Korma (pale blue – shade 677); Lipstick (pink – shade 680) and Sorbet (orange – shade 683)

Hook:

2.50mm (UK 12) crochet hook

Additional item:

Rigid metal ring, approximately 18cm (7in) in diameter

Tension:

Refer to Size above

What you have to do:

Make a selection of motifs, worked in the round, in each of five colours. Cover metal ring with double crochet worked in each colour. Work three lengths of chain and knot together for hanging loop. Use yarn tails to suspend motifs from ring.

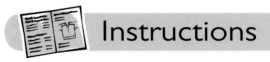 Instructions

Abbreviations:

ch = chain(s) **cm** = centimetre(s) **dc** = double crochet **dtr** = double treble **htr** = half treble **rep** = repeat **sp** = space **ss** = slip stitch **st(s)** = stitch(es) **tr** = treble

Note: At start of each motif, work over end of yarn to enclose it in first few sts then cut off tail.

At end of motif, fasten off and leave a long end of yarn, which will be used to suspend motif from ring.

SQUARE: (make 5 – 1 in each colour)

With 2.50mm (UK 12) hook make 5ch, join with a ss in first ch to form a ring.

1st round: 3ch (counts as 1tr), work 11tr in ring, join with a ss in 3rd of 3ch. 12 sts.

2nd round: 3ch, miss st at base of ch, *(2tr, 1dtr) in next

ch, *1ch, miss next st, (1tr, 2ch, 1tr) in next st, rep from * 6 times more, 1ch, join with a ss in 3rd of 5ch.

3rd round: Ss in first 2ch sp, 3ch, (1tr, 2ch, 2tr) in same sp, *1ch, (2tr, 2ch, 2tr) in next 2ch sp, rep from * 6 times more, 1ch, join with a ss in 3rd of 3ch.

4th round: Ss in next st and first 2ch sp, 3ch, 6tr in same sp, 1dc in next 1ch sp, *7tr in next 2ch sp, 1dc in next 1ch sp, rep from * 6 times more, join with a ss in 3rd of 3ch. Fasten off.

STAR: (make 5 – 1 in each colour)
With 2.50mm (UK 12) hook make 2ch and work 5dc in 2nd ch from hook, join with a ss in first dc.

1st round: 1ch (does not count as a st), 3dc in each of 5 sts, join with a ss in first dc. 15 sts.

2nd round: 1ch, *1dc in next dc, make 6ch, ss in 2nd ch from hook, 1dc in next ch, 1htr in next ch, 1tr in next ch, 1dtr in last ch, 1dtr in side of dc at base of 6ch, miss next 2 sts, rep from * 4 times more, join with a ss in first dc. Fasten off.

SCALLOPED CIRCLE: (make 5 – 1 in each colour)
With 2.50mm (UK 12) hook make 5ch, join with a ss in first ch to form a ring.

1st round: 2ch (counts as first htr), work 11htr in ring, join with a ss in 2nd of 2ch. 12 sts.

2nd round: 2ch, *2htr in next st, 1htr in next st, rep from * to last st, 2htr in last st, join with a ss in 2nd of 2ch. 18 sts.

3rd round: As 2nd. 27 sts.

4th round: *3ch, ss in each of next 2 sts, rep from * 12 times more, ss in last st. Fasten off.

SUNBURST: (make 5 – 1 in each colour)
With 2.50mm (UK 12) hook make 5ch, join with a ss in first ch to form a ring.

1st round: 1ch (does not count as a st), work 8dc in ring, join with a ss in first dc.

2nd round: 1ch, 3dc in each st to end, join with a ss in first dc. 24 sts.

3rd round: 1ch, 1dc in each st to end, join with a ss in first dc.

4th round: 1ch, 1dc in first st, *2dc in next st, 1dc in next st, rep from * 10 times more, 2dc in last st, join with a ss in first dc. 36 sts.

5th round: *5ch, ss in 2nd ch from hook, 1dc in next ch, 1htr in next ch, 1tr in last ch, miss next 2 sts, ss in next st, rep from * 11 times more. Fasten off.

st, (1dtr, 2tr) in next st (corner formed), 1tr in next st, rep from * twice more, (2tr, 1dtr) in next st, (1dtr, 2tr) in last st, join with a ss in 3rd of 3ch.

3rd round: 3ch, miss st at base of ch, 1tr in each of next 2 sts, *(2tr, 1dtr) in next st, (1dtr, 2tr) in next st (corner formed), 1tr in each of next 5 sts, rep from * twice more, (2tr, 1dtr) in next st, (1dtr, 2tr) in next st, 1tr in each of last 2 sts, join with a ss in 3rd of 3ch. Fasten off.

FLOWER: (make 5 – 1 in each colour)
With 2.50mm (UK 12) hook make 5ch, join with a ss in first ch to form a ring.

1st round: 3ch (counts as first tr), work 15tr in ring, join with a ss in 3rd of 3ch. 16 sts.

2nd round: 5ch (counts as 1tr, 2ch), 1tr in st at base of

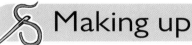

Making up

Press motifs.

To cover ring, knot yarn tails from all 5 balls around metal ring. Choose one colour to work with and, using 2.50mm (UK 12) hook and holding remaining 4 colours along edge of ring, work 20dc in ring so that ring and yarn tails are covered. Drop 1st colour and pick up 2nd colour. Work another 20dc in ring, covering ring and yarn tails as before. Rep all around ring, working each of 5 colours in turn and pushing sts up close together. When ring is completely covered, fasten off yarn in use. Cut off all other colours and weave in ends under sts.

With 2.50mm (UK 12) hook and your colour of choice, fasten yarn end to ring at a point where colour change occurs and make 50ch. Fasten off, leaving a long end. Rep twice more, spacing chains evenly around ring. Take all 3 yarn tails together and make 20ch, form this into a hanging loop for mobile and tie a knot at base of loop.

Hang up ring so that it is approximately at head height. Take motifs in turn and knot yarn tail loosely around ring at a point where colour change occurs; suspend a larger motif from base of hanging loop. Adjust length of each yarn tail so that motifs are suspended at different heights. Tie some motifs to base of other motifs. When you are happy with arrangement, tie knots more securely and trim off excess yarn tails.

Index

Acknowledgements

Managing Editor: Clare Churly
Editors: Lesley Malkin and Eleanor van Zandt
Senior Art Editor: Juliette Norsworthy
Designer: Janis Utton
Assistant Production Manager: Caroline Alberti